So You Want to Be a Philanthropist

D1444278

How to Choose,
Set Up and Manage a
Successful Family Foundation

Julia A. Kittross

ISBN: 978-1492722335

Book jacket design by DesignConceptsLA.com

Printed in the United States of America

ACKNOWLEDGMENTS

To Kym Belden, who said I could;
to my husband, Stuart Schnell,
who without, I could not have crossed the finish line.

And thanks to all those who made this book possible: Joyce White, Diane Kaplan, Doug Bauer, John M. Kittross and David Kittross read early drafts and made great suggestions. Laverne Woods, Attorney-at-Law, reviewed the legal sections and greatly improved their accuracy. Alice Porter helped turn gnarly sentences into understandable ones and Matt Schnell aided in finding the typos I'd missed.

And thanks to all of my clients and other foundation donors, trustees and staff who shared their experiences so this book can be useful for those following in their footsteps.

Note: any errors remain those of the author, and should not be ascribed to those generous people listed above.

TABLE OF CONTENTS

PREFACE

After decades of working with philanthropists, foundation staff and trustees, and nonprofit organizations, I had noticed a gap in the information available for those thinking about creating a private family foundation. There are articles and books and organizations totally dedicated to this audience. But I couldn't find a resource that provided what I like to call, "a comprehensive introduction."

Yes, this descriptor may be considered an oxymoron. But this book is designed to be just such a "comprehensive introduction." It touches on almost everything private foundation-related, but doesn't go terribly deep into any one thing. *So You Want To Be a Philanthropist* allows you to think about whether a private family foundation is the right choice, and if so, how to start, organize and manage such a foundation. More importantly, perhaps, it asks lots of questions that you need to answer as you consider how to move ahead.

Resources are numerous and often cited, and for those of you who decide a to launch a private foundation (or are unhappy with your past results attempting to manage one), this book is meant to get you on the right track.

Of course there are many consultants willing to help you along the way (including Philanthropy Sherpas!), but for those of you who like to learn on their own, *So You Want To Be a Philanthropist* may be just the right tool for you.

—*Julia A. Kittross*
Philanthropy Sherpas
www.PhilanthropySherpas.com

INTRODUCTION

I magine the following...

Your estate planner has recommended that you form a private foundation for tax purposes. You've always been interested in giving to good causes and you really want to help your community theater grow, or build a new wing on the local hospital, or adopt a 6th grade class so everyone with a B average can later go to college. You admire your neighbor who has a family foundation and what she's accomplished through it. A foundation? What a great idea! "Let's do it," you say to your attorney.

Schreeeeech!!!!

May I please suggest you put on the brakes and read the first three chapters of this book?

I believe in the power of philanthropy and the potential of planned and thoughtful giving to improve individual lives and society as a whole. If you don't think the same way, you probably wouldn't be reading this book. Nonetheless, I often suggest to clients that they *not* set up their own private foundation solely at the suggestion of their certified public accountant or estate-planning attorney. I hear you ask, "But don't they know if I should do so?" I don't want to earn the enmity of these professionals — honestly, some of my best friends are lawyers and accountants — but they may *primarily* be thinking about your tax or estate-planning situation when making this suggestion. What you need at this juncture is the big picture.

Sometimes philanthropy is done purely for altruistic reasons, but often there are other motivations. When you organize unwanted household items to send off to Goodwill, there is a sense of helping others. But you, too, benefit from the act in another way — less clutter to care for. When you support an after-school program for disadvantaged children, you like to feel you're doing good. But you also recognize that you are benefiting from a social order that provides children with activities that are more productive than hanging out on street corners. A contribution to an environmental group, you hope, will help build a better, cleaner, and more attractive world for you and your current and future children and grandchildren to enjoy.

In many ways you are already a philanthropist. You donate, serve on a board, even tithe. Now, however, it's been suggested that you set up a private foundation as a means of organizing your charitable giving. Your accountant and estate-planning attorney are thinking about taxes, and that is their job. But there are alternatives to a foundation that might better suit your specific goals.

What I *am* saying is that choosing the structure of your giving — a private foundation, donor advised fund, personal checkbook gifting, transfers of property or some other form — should not be *solely* based on tax considerations. I've met many philanthropists who have created a private foundation (at not insignificant expense) only to dismantle it years later when they realized it didn't meet their needs.

This book is designed for those who want to intentionally and thoughtfully organize their eleemosynary[1] impulses — especially those who eventually decide to go ahead with a private foundation. The following chapters will outline a number of options that you should consider, and advice on choosing the best one, before you sign on the dotted line.

---

[1] Another term lovingly used by the IRS to describe philanthropic activities.

1 | LET'S GO SHOPPING:
OPTIONS FOR ORGANIZING
YOUR GIVING

Before we discuss in detail what philanthropic vehicles are available to you, let me explain what is usually meant by "nonprofit organizations." Philanthropists want to make change happen. They tend to do so by providing resources to empower 501(c)(3) public charity exempt organizations doing work that serve their communities. Section 501(c)(3) is the section of the U.S. Internal Revenue Code that describes charitable organizations that are exempt from federal income tax. This includes the private foundation you're thinking about, and others, known as public charities that have proven to the IRS's satisfaction that they are supported by the public or conduct certain types of activities that benefit the public.

Donors can give directly to any 501(c)(3) public charity in good standing with the IRS and receive a charitable contribution tax deduction. You can also receive a deduction for gifts to local governments (think school districts, the local department of health, or public libraries, as long as their policies allow it) and religious entities.

There are other types of 501(c) organizations — 29 in total — that are exempt from various federal income taxes, but donations to them generally don't provide the donor a tax deduction. For instance, 501(c)(4) organizations can attempt to influence campaigns to a limited degree and lobby for legislation. 501(c)(3) nonprofits, however, are prohibited from supporting political candidates and operate with restrictions on the extent to which they can lobby. Another example of one of these 29 categories of exempt organizations is the 501(c)(8), which are fraternal beneficiary associations like the Rotary Club.[2] If you aren't sure your gift will receive a tax deduction, ask the organization. Or your attorney.

Now on to the choices you have to organize your giving.

Bequests and Planned Giving

This is the easiest. Choose your favorite nonprofit(s), include a bequest in your will, and wait to die. No work, no muss, no fuss, and a very happy nonprofit may send someone to your memorial service to show its thanks.

Checkbook Philanthropy

Writing personal checks to the charities of your choice is an easy, low-cost way to be philanthropic. And if you want to focus your giving, treat those appeals you receive like grant proposals. Get off the mailing lists of organizations you'd rather not support so you have more resources to focus on those that you do. Checkbook philanthropy can be extremely sophisticated if you wish it to be.

Donor Advised Funds

Donor advised funds (DAFs) are an option for many donors who don't want to deal with all of the paperwork and pretty much know what cause or organization they want to give to. My family has a donor advised fund and it perfectly serves its purpose to honor my mother and allow my brother, father and me to argue (enjoyably) each year over what grants we can make to reflect her values.

DAFs are available through community foundations, Jewish federations, and through charitable gift funds created by investment companies, banks, and other entities. Some of these are religiously focused, and some make money from the services they provide. Which should you choose? The DAFs have differing minimum donations and charge varied fees; they also invest the funds using assorted investment

---

[2] From http://www.irs.gov/pub/irs-pdf/p557.pdf

philosophies. Community foundations will be able to share their expertise about the needs and providers in your geographic region while the national gift funds are more like checkbooks. But they do ensure that the funds go only to qualified 501(c)(3) organizations.

The thing to remember in both cases is that your gift is made as soon as you provide the minimum amount (or more) to the DAF — that is, in itself, an account owned by a 501(c)(3) public charity. Your tax deduction is taken not when you recommend where the gifts are to go, but when you open or add to your DAF. Note too that a DAF is just that — advised. Since you've given the gift to the non-profit community foundation or charitable fund, it is *its* board of directors who officially approve where the grants go. As a DAF donor, you may only advise where you want donations to go; realistically it will go there as long as it is both legal and ethical to do so.

Lastly, DAFs pay no excise tax (which private foundations do; see below), don't cost high legal set-up fees, aren't subject to the 5% payout obligation (also required of private foundations) and free you from the accounting and paperwork involved in grantmaking. There are very large DAFs that can function as *de facto* foundations — even with staff. And many smaller ones are effective ways to distribute donations with significantly lower costs, leaving you with a larger gift pool.

Giving Circles

Giving circles[3] are typically informal groups of unrelated people who share a particular issue or concern they wish to address or strategy they wish to use via group grantmaking. Giving circles are not, unlike most of the others listed here, a legal structure and are a form of checkbook philanthropy practiced with other like-minded people. These can be quite fun, create great learning opportunities, and make for rewarding philanthropy. They are usually managed in a one-person, one-vote manner, majority rules, so there is no question about decisions.

Giving circles are usually created around a specific issue. Even friends who gather quarterly for dinner, throw $25 or $50 checks into a pot, and then determine together where the money is to be donated are giving circles.

---

[3] Rather dated but still useful information about giving circles is available at www.givingcircles.org and at http://www.givingforum.org/s_forum/sec.asp?CID=611&DID=2661

Public Foundations

Public foundations are public charities and are somewhat similar to giving circles except that they are 501(c)(3) public charities and they raise dollars for their grantmaking budget not only from individuals but also from other groups including private foundations and corporations. Think of them like any nonprofit public charity (that must meet the public support test of the IRS proving they are supported by the public and not just one donor) whose mission is to make grants to others through donations by its members. Note that cash contributions to all public charities, including public foundations, allow for a maximum deduction of 50% of your adjusted gross income (AGI), vs. the 30% allowed for contributions to a private foundation or 30% (vs. 20% to private foundations) for gifts of property.

You may wonder where to find public foundations. Some of you may have heard of Social Venture Partners — this is a public foundation. So too are many women's funds, most of which focus their giving on women and girls (although not all — see Washington Women's Foundation, for example). Social justice funds[4] are frequently structured in this manner as well.

Supporting Organizations

If you know that what you mostly want to do is to provide advice and support to one nonprofit that you care deeply about, in addition to checkbook philanthropy and giving through a donor advised fund, you could consider setting up a supporting organization, which is not a private foundation but a charity that "supports" another charity. There are three types of supporting organizations (Types I – III), each of which have rules and regulations that require an attorney's involvement. Supporting organizations allow the donor to avoid private foundation status (and many of the regulations) but the donor may not control them.

---

[4] Google® "social justice funds" and several will come up; they tend to be geographically based.

Private *Operating* Foundations

Lastly, you may decide that you want to be engaged in the work itself. But you don't want to create a new public charity that would require you to raise funds and meet the public support test of the IRS. So instead, you fund the creation of a private operating foundation that must spend a defined amount in active operations, not grants.[5] Some examples include operating a zoo, museum, or research facility or providing direct services. Specific examples include the Getty Trust, the Casey Family Programs, and the Flintridge Center.

Your maximum deduction for a contribution to a private operating foundation is the same as to public charities — up to 50% of your adjusted gross income. Thirty percent of your AGI is the maximum deduction allowed for contributions to a private foundation (for gifts of cash). Private operating foundations are also subject to a 1-2% excise tax on their investment income (as are private foundations; see below). All other tax law requirements for a private foundation apply.

The one option that is missing so far is the one your attorney suggested to you back on page 1. Read the following chapter for the details about private foundations.

---

[5] See *IRS Definition of a Private Operating Foundation* at http://www.irs.gov/Charities-&-Non-Profits/Private-Foundations/Definition-of-Private-Operating-Foundation

2 | AND IN THIS CORNER, THE PRIVATE FOUNDATION

This is the organized philanthropic structure your attorney suggested you create at the beginning of this book. The long history of the Rockefeller and Ford Foundations, as well as the more recent establishment of the Bill & Melinda Gates Foundation, has made private foundations the most well known type of philanthropic structure.

But private foundations operate under a number of restrictions and strict rules that may not be something you want to take on. Some of these are listed below.

A Confusing Term

The term "private foundation" may be confusing. It is the legal term for foundations that make grants including:

1. Family foundations (those with the donor or his/her descendants involved)
2. Corporate foundations (funded by a corporation or other business)
3. Independent foundations (no family involved, although there may have been at one time)

Private operating foundations, which I mentioned in the previous chapter, are also private foundations, in spite of the fact that they make expenditures primarily for direct charitable programs rather than for grants. Every type of private foundation is required to follow the same IRS regulations (barring the exceptions for private operating foundations noted in Chapter 1).

To further perplex us, many public charities that are seeking public support call themselves foundations. The Children's Hospital Foundation, for instance, isn't a grantmaking private foundation — it's a public charity — but since the word "foundation" has both a legal definition and a different meaning in common parlance, the Children's Hospital Foundation may use the term as it wishes.

Tax Deductibility

Direct gifts to charities and donor advised funds generally receive more favorable tax treatment than a donation to your private foundation. Contributions to public charities, including DAFs and Public foundations, allow donors to take a federal income tax deduction up to 50% of adjusted gross income for cash contributions, and up to 30% of AGI for appreciated securities and some other forms of investments. The tax deductions for donations to private foundations are generally less — 20% to 30% of AGI depending on the form of the donation. The type of contribution also can affect whether your deduction will be limited to your tax basis or its fair market value.[6] The idea is to allow those who give directly to nonprofits more of a tax deduction. Tax law is complex and there are many exceptions and rules that cannot be generalized; do talk to your tax attorney or CPA.

Distribution Requirements

Five percent of the value of your net invested assets that are not used directly in charitable activities must be distributed annually. Note that many — but not all — expenses necessary to manage the foundation can

---

[6] Bruce R. Hopkins and Jody Blazek, Private Foundations: Tax Law and Compliance, EBook Section 2.2: "Funding a Foundation," John Wiley and Sons, 2008.

be included[7] and that's true in a "down" market as well as an "up" one. Therefore, it is possible to eat into your principal over time if you are unable to make returns of 8+% on the corpus of money, since you must allow for inflation, add your investment fees and another 1 – 2% for taxes on top of the 5% "payout." There is a way to average your payout over several years, and you can give more than 5% in one year and "bank" that extra for future years. But still, you have a mandated budget — that 6% to 7% the IRS requires you to spend — that is somewhat of a moving figure until your accountant determines the value of your previous year's assets. I've run into many foundations panicking at the end of the year trying to get money out the door, which does not guarantee sound and well thought-out choices.

If you plan on funding your giving by a gift of non-income producing property that is not easily converted to cash, placing it in a private foundation can make the requirement that 5% be distributed annually even more of a challenge.

The Cost Factor

It costs money to start a private foundation. The 30-page "Application for Recognition of Exemption IRS Form 1023" isn't particularly fun to fill out. Add articles of incorporation, by-laws, conflict of interest, whistleblower and other policies, and it can cost more than a few thousand dollars in set-up fees as well as fees charged by attorneys, investment advisers, custodians and CPAs.

You'll also need a good attorney on retainer — or at least on speed dial — to review any out-of-the-ordinary gifts you may wish to make. Attorneys are also useful to help ensure that you and all other "disqualified persons"[8] aren't violating the "self-dealing" laws (see Chapter 13 for details). These rules are squirrely because transactions can appear to be favorable to the foundation but still be considered self-dealing, so you really can't get away without the advice of a good attorney.

---

[7] The most notable expenses that cannot be included in your payout calculations are investment fees, any other costs related to the oversight of investments (such as the board's investment committee meeting expenses), and excise taxes.

[8] Disqualified persons include any officer, director or trustee; their spouses, ancestors and family (down to the great grandchildren and their spouses); substantial contributors (2% or more of total contributions or bequests in a fiscal year, or the creator of a trust whether or not their donations exceed 2% in a year); any corporation, partnership or trust or estate of which a disqualified person owns more than 35%.

Please be aware that your family or business attorney — sometimes even your estate planning attorney — may not be familiar with the nuances of private foundation law, because it's a very specialized field.

Excise Tax on Investment income
Yes, you have to pay taxes

As mentioned above, a private foundation is required to pay a 1% to 2% excise tax annually on its investment income, including any capital gains. There are ways to keep the tax at the 1%. One way is to make sure that your current year payout exceeds the average payout of the previous five years.

Another way to limit your foundation's tax liability is to limit its investment income by funding it with "pass-through" donations you make to the foundation when you commit to grants or other direct expenses. Individuals choosing to fund their foundation from income often have widely varying income or net worth from year to year, or derive much of their income from investments, such as real estate. The down side is that the individual donor receives tax benefits only from the amount given each year rather than that which would be realized by making a larger transfer of assets to the foundation's control at one time.

Others Are Watching

You must file an annual tax return (called a Form 990-PF, which stands for private foundation) that, unlike the regular Form 1040, is available to the public online and on demand, so your giving (and your investments and expenses running your foundation) will only be anonymous if you form an LLC or grantor trust (another legal expense), while in other options you merely have to state the gift should be kept anonymous. Money gifted to your own private foundation no longer actually belongs to you — you become a steward of those funds to serve the public. As a result, reporters, lawmakers, and generally nosy folks have a right to know what you're doing with "their" money. While it might have your name on it and you can choose your grant recipients, anyone can make an unwelcome public stir about what you do.

Time Consuming

Managing the day-to-day activities of a private foundation takes time — there's no way around it. You can hire people to do much of what you don't want to do, but then there's less money available for grantmaking.

As a member of the philanthropic community you also have a responsibility to share what you do and what you learn with your peers and the nonprofits that rely on your largesse. This means, at minimum, a website. An annual report or digest of what you've learned, activities you performed and grants you made should be posted on that website. And your decision-making system and criteria for making grants — and how to apply for them — should be clear and known.

Get the idea? Creating your own private foundation takes work, costs money, and doesn't generate the best tax deduction out there. So before you choose that route, you owe it to yourself and your potential grant recipients to explore other options that may meet your goals more effectively.

After All This, There *Are* Reasons to Start a Private Foundation

Let's list some of the reasons *for* choosing to establish a private foundation:

- *Lot's o' dough?* If you have a large amount of money to invest in philanthropy from a liquidity event, or you know that you'll have significant resources over time that you'd like to devote to philanthropy, a private foundation makes sense. There is no strict minimum amount of dollars you should have for a foundation. It depends on what you want to accomplish. But for small funds, unless you know they'll grow in the future — at your passing, for instance — you should at least consider some of the other ideas in Chapter 2 before you decide on the private foundation choice.

- *Are you a control-freak?* OK, you don't have to be a freak. But those who choose a foundation often cite issues of control. Private foundations offer the donor and his or her fellow trustees full control, within the limits of the law and the Internal Revenue Code, of where that foundation's donations will go, the strategies you'll use, and the investment policies you'll implement for the stewardship of the foundation's assets. Of course, so does checkbook philanthropy.

- *Do you want your family to work together?* The Association of Small Foundations says that family foundations can "engender an ethic of community-mindedness among family members and…strengthen family ties by engaging relatives in a constructive, positive endeavor."[9] Many family foundation donors and trustees cite this as a major reason for their foundation's existence.

- *Are you greatly attached to your community or want to give back some of the good fortune you received from a region?* By creating a foundation to serve your hometown or where you or your family earned your wealth, you are announcing a public commitment to that geographic area that can influence others to do the same.

- *Do you want your philanthropy to live on into the foreseeable future?* Most foundations are created "in perpetuity," or forever. This concept of permanence appeals to many. Not only could your children be engaged in the foundation's work, but their children, and so on. Think about the older large foundations today: the Ford, Rockefeller, and MacArthur foundations, for instance. Now, more than a century since their inceptions, they are still generously investing in society and have donated many times their original asset value.[10] [11] Most community foundations do offer versions of multi-generational options and even perpetuity

---

[9] http://www.smallfoundations.org/about/members/importance/why-a-foundation/

[10] Note: there is a small, but growing trend to consider spending out of existence within the lifetime of the donor or the next generation. This choice is made usually because of a belief that more money now will make a difference in solving a social problem, rather than holding back smaller amounts over time. Also some donors choose this to have the joy of seeing the results of their philanthropy during their own lifetimes. For example, the Bill & Melinda Gates Foundation intends to spend out within 50 years of the death of Bill and Melinda. See Duke University's "spend down" library with information and case studies on why people have done so and what they've learned: http://cspcs.sanford.duke.edu/spenddown_library.

[11] Of course there are those who believe that sunsetting may be the best option for the Ford, Rockefeller and MacArthur Foundations, since it is their opinion that the foundations have moved away from their donors' original visions.

succession plans for your DAF, if you endow the fund with that purpose in mind.

- *Do you want your profession to be the practice of philanthropy?* Establishing a structure that allows for employees (whether that's you, unpaid, or someone else, including another family member, who can be paid a reasonable salary) may be a good choice if you want philanthropy to be your career or that of a family member or other person you'd like to involve. Another advantage of choosing to manage a private foundation is that there is a philanthropic support industry designed to provide you, your fellow board members, and any staff you may have with career development opportunities and peer support.

- *Are you interested in using the power of an organization to advance your mission?* It's often easier to collaborate, convene people, and play other leadership roles with an organization behind you. An invitation to a gathering from the Jane Smith Family Foundation will likely receive more RSVPs than one from Jane Smith, unless she's well known individually.

- *Do you wish you had an easy answer to people who approach you for funding at cocktail parties?* With a foundation you can say, "Here's the website address for my foundation. There is a process and set of criteria for its grantmaking, but please go ahead and take a look to see if you think there's a fit." This is harder to deal with if you're writing personal checks for your contributions.

- *Do you want to see your family and family name respected over the years?* Who hasn't heard of the Rockefeller or Carnegie, or some other foundation named after an individual or family that faced, shall we say, public relations problems? Such foundations often have a far more savory reputation than the original donor.

- *Do you just like the idea of having a foundation with your name attached?*[12]
  People give for many reasons: guilt, honoring their parents, creating a family legacy, improving society, crafting an estate plan that takes advantage of all options. A private foundation, with or without your family, may be just what you want.

Now you know more than you ever wanted to know about the different ways you can structure your charitable giving. And believe me, your attorney will likely tell you about still more! How do you choose among these options? Let's step back a bit and think more broadly about the purpose of philanthropy, ways to try it out, and questions that, if answered, can point you more solidly in the right direction.

---

[12] Note: some people don't want their foundation named after them. This helps keep their activities at least somewhat less known in circles where philanthropy isn't a common topic of discussion. And for some, naming their foundation something inocuous like the Sunshine Foundation has to do with safety issues or protecting their children from embarrassment: "Jeez, you must be rich. I saw your name on the wall at the hospital the other day."

3 | HOW TO CHOOSE?

First Practice, Then Reflect

B efore you choose your giving structure, I suggest you put your toe in the water of organized giving to see if you like it. You don't have to do everything overnight.

The easiest way is to join a network of individuals giving jointly such as Social Venture Partners or a Women's fund or simply write more targeted or larger personal checks. It feels just as good, and it may *do* just as much good as a check drawn on a private foundation account.

If you like what you're doing, ask yourself: "Is this enough? Or do I want to do more?" One way to reflect on how to organize your generosity is to think about *why* you wish to do so. Is it only because your tax attorney or CPA brought it up? Just what is your goal?

OK, Just What *Is* Your Goal?

Answer this: What do you want to accomplish through your organized philanthropy? Look over the suggestions below. You may acknowledge that more than one fits you, or you may have thought of other reasons on your own.

- To "give back" to the community that supported the origination of your wealth?

- To encourage your children to learn about the issues and problems across town so they gain a deeper understanding of the world around them?
- To make change in a system that seems broken? Take your pick: education, mental health, health care access, entrenched poverty, arts and culture, etc.
- To provide charity to ease suffering?
- To strengthen nonprofits so they can better achieve their goals?
- To provide yourself, spouse, child, or grandchild with an opportunity to enter a rewarding profession by managing the foundation?
- To test your belief that you might have an idea about how to fix something?
- To encourage your friends, family, and business colleagues to give more by leading the way?
- To bask in the warmth of gratitude and recognition for your philanthropy?
- To honor your parents or someone else by supporting what they cared for in their day?
- To ensure your favorite nonprofit is sufficiently resourced for a long and fruitful life with a rainy day or an innovation fund?
- To see your family's name on the local theater building or university gym?
- To engage your family in a joint endeavor?
- To become a community leader?

You may select a combination of two or more of the above options or develop an idea for something entirely different. Don't pick one because you think you *should* practice philanthropy for one reason over another. Pick *your* reasons with care, because your choices here will affect your philanthropy in significant ways.

People dedicate resources for the public good for many different reasons. All of them end up with a community that profits from the gifts and the on-going commitment of resources being invested over time. So be honest and identify why you want to be a philanthropist by determining what you want to accomplish. Form will follow function —

what structure you should use will become more obvious the clearer you are with yourself about your goals.

Ginny Esposito of the National Center for Family Philanthropy crafted many of the following questions. They should be answered before you choose which way to go.

Are You In This For the Long Haul?

Is gifting in a focused manner something you want to do only during your lifetime? For the next ten years? Or do you want your children or other people to carry on your philanthropic purpose or create their own giving legacy?

If your interest is to focus your giving during your lifetime (or soon thereafter), think twice before creating a private foundation. Thoughtful checkbook giving, joining a giving circle, or starting a DAF would most likely be the better choices. If your answer is to create a philanthropic entity to last into the following generations, a private foundation can be considered. If you only want to go one generation or so, a DAF may still be a good choice.

How Much Money Do You Plan to Commit to Philanthropy?

You may hear from advisers of various sorts that you need to have at least $1 million — or more likely $10 to $50 million — to launch a private foundation. Bull pucky. The amount of money is much less important than the answers to what you want to accomplish. There are, however, economies of scale, and you should consider how willing you are to pay for the administrative resources needed to manage a foundation.

You may only have $25,000 now to invest in philanthropy; but at your death you want a portion of your estate to fund the foundation to a larger extent. A private foundation may be a perfectly appropriate choice in this case. Your main goal may be to provide your children an opportunity to build a career in philanthropy. If so, a private foundation may be a fine option even if you haven't tens or hundreds of millions to fund a foundation in perpetuity.

Then again, if you don't see your resources increasing much beyond several thousand dollars a year, sticking with checkbook philanthropy is likely the most efficient way to go. It may not, however, be the most effective.

Sometimes, even a small amount of money can make a big difference. For example, a theater student at my *alma mater* gave a few hundred dollars to install a toilet backstage, and generations of future theater students blessed his foresight.

Do You Want Other Family Members to Be Involved?

One of the typical reasons you may hear people say why they started their family's foundation was to "bring their family together." May I be so bold as to suggest six "do not" rules about starting a family foundation?

1. Do not expect your foundation to automatically make your children like each other.
2. Do not expect your foundation to automatically make you and your children get along.
3. Do not expect your foundation to prevent your child from becoming a ski bum or a starving artist.
4. Do not expect your foundation to allow you and your children or grandchildren (or your parents or siblings, for that matter) to suddenly behave and communicate like adults.
5. Do not expect your children and grandchildren to be interested in your causes or to continue funding what you cared about after you're gone.
6. Do not expect your brother to suddenly respect you.

Once you realize that none of these will *inevitably* come true without effort, thinking about your potential foundation goes in a new direction. Do you want family members involved?

Do You Only Want to Give Scholarships?

A common philanthropic desire is to fashion a scholarship or multiple scholarships to help low-income kids go to college, or honor one's *alma mater* by giving it scholarship funding in your past field of study. Be aware: scholarship grants programs managed by private foundations require advance IRS approval of grantmaking. But you can always donate the money to the educational institution, community foundation, or public charity (Dollars for Scholars, The United Negro College Fund or the College Success Foundation, for instance) and let *them* run the application process instead. You can make that donation directly to the educational institution or scholarship public charity from your checkbook (the easiest), set up a scholarship fund at the local community foundation, or you're your private foundation manage the process (the most expensive choice if scholarships are all you plan to fund).

If, however, you want your family to manage and participate in choosing the scholarship recipients, a private foundation can do so. Just be aware of the extra time and cost of designing your process, having the IRS approve that process, and then poring through the applications to follow.

How Much Time and Effort Do You Want to Put Into Philanthropy?

Unless you plan to give gifts to the same dozen nonprofits a year, you will be spending some time at this endeavor. You will be reviewing nonprofits, which can change their goals and procedures as easily as you can, for good reasons and bad. Signing checks and letters. Keeping track of your grants over time. Learning what was accomplished each year by those you support. Filing your 990-PF annual tax return. Overseeing your investment returns and establishing an investment policy. (Some have trustees who actually *do* the investing rather than hiring someone else.) Holding board or trustee meetings. All this is a minimum.

You may decide to spend even more time practicing philanthropy. Going on "site visits," e.g., meeting with the nonprofit leaders at their office or place where they provide services. Learning about "best practices" in the fields you fund. Teaching your children or grandchildren about philanthropy. Determining how to best evaluate your efforts. Sharing your results through reports, a website, or attending grantmaker gatherings. Investing the foundation's assets in projects that build and improve the community — this is called mission-related investing (MRI). And there are more activities you *could* do as a philanthropist.

So answer this: How much time in week, or a month, do you wish to dedicate to your philanthropic activities? Two hours a week? Twenty hours a month? Are you making this your second career or enjoyable hobby? Or is this an annual endeavor with your family designed to do some good and feel good but not take too much time except for the end-of-year gathering? By determining this, you will know better how to focus your giving, decide on the size of grants you wish to make, whether you or someone else in your family or someone you hire will take on the administration of the foundation, and even whether you should set up a foundation at all.

HOW A FOUNDATION ACTUALLY DID HELP A FAMILY ENJOY WORKING TOGETHER

After listing all the "don't expect" warnings above, I'd be remiss if I didn't note that family foundations can bring families closer together.

A family foundation that consisted of very busy siblings, their spouses and their father had treated their family foundation much like a checkbook, by equally dividing the amount available and allowing each board member to suggest a recipient for that amount (although all had to agree). It's not uncommon for a private foundation to allow each board member a certain amount of grant dollars to designate; but in this case, the entire grant budget was divvied up. Desiring a more connected manner of giving but leery of the amount of time that might take, they experimented with some of the grantmaking budget. Setting aside $100,000, they determined that all board members could recommend a recipient, after which the board would meet to narrow it down to two. After site visits to the two finalists, they voted on the one that received the entire $100,000.

They enjoyed the interaction together so much that they decided to undertake the joint grantmaking process in future years.

Do You Want to Play With Others Or Go It Alone?

The easiest decisions are those made by one person. Once another enters the picture it can become complicated and time-consuming. While some states have legal requirements for a certain minimum number of directors or trustees,[13] I've had clients where the foundation is primarily managed by one of the spouses involved — and indeed the State of Washington requires only one director. Add your children, brother or sister, niece or nephew, or even your parents, and the decision-making process becomes increasingly difficult.

Of course you may be considering a foundation for the purpose of working with your family. Or to allow your children or grandchildren a

---

[13] If the private foundation is set up as a nonprofit corporation the board members are called directors; they are called trustees if it is set up as a trust.

venue to labor together under the guidance of shared values. You may like doing things in groups or teams and recognize that it can be the back-and-forth discussions, disagreements, and dialogues that make for interesting sessions. It also can spread the workload to avoid one person becoming overwhelmed.

Deciding that you want others to participate is a little more complex than just saying, "Hey, son, I've created a family foundation and I want you to be a trustee." Think ahead about what this means.

Do you still want the foundation to do what you, the donor, want? Do you expect the kids, other relatives or non-family members — friends, experts, community representatives, legal/financial advisors, religious leader, etc. — you invite to participate to defer mostly to you because after all, it was your money? Or are you willing to make decisions as a group, democratically, through consensus or vote-taking? Does this mean decisions about grants? Or about focus areas, grantmaking methodologies, or investment policies? You'll have happier campers around the fire if you allow them to have a real voice in all matters. But then you may see your ideas voted down and not like that feeling. Also, everyone involved needs to know the conflict of interest and other IRS rules, since they share your responsibility over the corpus, and you'll likely have to educate them.

If working collaboratively is important to you, both foundations and DAFs can join with others in learning and grantmaking activities, such as pooled funds. And public foundations and informal giving circles are collaboration personified.

These questions have been designed to help you evaluate the various philanthropic vehicles available to you. Be aware that you can choose more than one. For example, many private foundation founders also has a DAF (see story box below) for those infrequent anonymous gifts or for when they are unable to meet their payout by the end of the year because they're immersed in foundation strategic planning, changing their grantmaking direction, studying up on the best approaches and otherwise need more time to thoughtfully distribute their funds.

The following very short chapter goes beyond how to decide — to making the choice of vehicle itself.

YOU CAN HAVE MORE THAN ONE VEHICLE
(and change your direction)

Shaula Massena had a big, hairy, audacious vision: to address issues of racial and gender inequality. Forming the Massena Foundation seemed like a good thing to do when she and her husband retired as two IT workers who benefited from the early dot.com boom in the '90s. The foundation allowed Shaula to learn about solutions to problems that she, herself, had faced as a woman, and those she only understood at a surface level, since her race is Caucasian. By inviting members of communities of color to participate in determining the foundation's guidelines and to make recommendations for funding, Shaula took on a more daring challenge than many philanthropists would in their early days.

After a few years, however, she made a change. She explained, "the administrative hassle of a community advisory board was too high and my ability to feel a sense of connection & impact across a big scattershot portfolio was too low, so the solutions were to 1) stop doing the community application process and 2) switch to fewer, larger grants. The relationships & learning from the community advisory board period definitely impacted the set of relationships I ultimately sustained."

She also decided to modify her focus. "The shift to focusing on economic development and impact investing was driven by a growing sense that you can't grant empowerment, you can only support people in earning it for themselves."

Up against a liquidity event and the 30% adjusted gross income deduction cap to private foundations, she decided to also create a donor advised fund. She chose ImpactAssets (which offers donors a way to both invest in mission-related investments and, if they desire, make grants) through which the bulk of her loans and other social investments now flow. She is happy with and uses both her giving vehicles now, although won't rule out merging them in the future.

4 | IT'S TIME TO PICK
YOUR GIVING VEHICLE

You now have basic information about most philanthropic structures, more details about private foundations, and you've answered several questions to help you narrow your choice. Time to pick which philanthropic entity you want! Comparisons and suggestions of "if you want to do this, then that is a good choice" have been sprinkled throughout the previous chapters. Let's review.

No doubt, you can see that some choices are easier than others. Bequests are the easiest, but then you don't get to see the results of your donation. If you simply wish to maximize your tax benefits on an annual basis, checkbook giving or donor advised funds are very attractive. They also allow for flexibility. Give to the local animal shelter and youth sports league one year, and then send it all to procure and maintain a valued community green space the next. This is easy — you just open your checkbook. But there are drawbacks. Your email and mailbox will always be full of requests, and while the personal approach can be nice, it can also put a damper on a social event you wished to enjoy without being approached for funding.

There are gradations of choices. A giving circle sounds like great fun. And it can be, whether you're directing small donations or large. An evening with friends, pooling some money, discussing shared values and things you'd like to change in the world, along with the relative merits of those charities focused on making those changes. Yes, giving circles (particularly with good food and good wine) are very attractive. You still receive your tax benefit, but you don't control the outcome. It's a group process.

With public foundations you may give up a bit more control. Think of it as a large giving circle, but instead of a handful of close friends combining resources, funds are gathered from a larger variety of individuals and other sources. Systems are more complex. And when the time comes to determine where the donations are to be directed it may be one-person-one-vote, but it also could be the decision of a subcommittee. You'll obviously have less influence on where the donations go — a lot less than simply writing a check yourself and sending it to the local theatre troupe.

And then there are supporting organizations and private operating foundations. These are typically chosen for very specific reasons. But if it's work you enjoy and you want to fund it, then great! Create a supporting organization to your community foundation or to the local women's shelter and focus your support on mental health counseling for the residents. Or open a reptile zoo, hire expert staff, and bring kids in to learn about snakes.

As this discussion has proceeded, I've been keenly aware of one belief that I hold dear that I may not have made clear to you:

PHILANTHROPY SHOULD BE FUN!

Have I made private foundations seem scary or burdensome? I hope not. I love family foundations. I've helped create them, helped define and refine their missions, helped focus and refocus their grantmaking practices, and helped resolve their internal (sometimes family) disputes and staffing issues. They work! They work for the individuals and families who have thoughtfully and intentionally formed them, and they often work for the generations that follow.

On the other hand, sometimes they don't work, at least not as you had hoped when you launched them. Take a good hard look back at Chapter 3. What *are* your goals? Your values? What will a private foundation do for you? Thinking this way isn't small minded or self-serving. The act of giving should be fun and rewarding and trust me, it can be.

The beginning of this book has focused on the first decision you had to face: how to structure your giving. The remainder of this book focuses primarily on important things for private family foundations to keep in mind as they form, make granting decisions, review their work, alter course, pass to the next generation, and grow. It may also be useful and interesting to those who have chosen one of the other philanthropic vehicles available

5 | GRANTMAKING: AN OVERVIEW

Start With Values and Goals

As you have been working and thinking your way through this book, you have been examining your values and goals in order to select the philanthropic vehicle that will serve you best. Applying this same approach will lead you to a set of criteria and strategies to make good decisions about your grantmaking. You can do this yourself, with your family, or with the help of a good facilitator.

There are practical things to consider (website, tracking system, office space, staffing), as well as operational decisions such as choosing which types of grants you'll make (see Chapter 8) and whether to accept proposals (see Chapter 10). But first, let's revisit your values and goals as they affect how you choose to disperse and invest your philanthropic dollars.

What do you as an individual, couple, or family value? Compassion for the needy? Helping people to help themselves? Access to education as a way out of poverty? Creativity? Service? Generosity? Social justice?

A number of philanthropy advisers have developed resources (lists of values, photos or cards) that make it easier for you to choose your top three or four.[14] Having a conversation as a family about your individual

---

[14] Two organizations, the Philanthropic Initiative and 21/64, and the book *Inspired Philanthropy* by Tracy Gary are three of these resources. You can also find a variety of examples on the Internet.

values can be a very rewarding and enlightening experience. Finding among those individual values the ones shared by the whole group can be exhilarating. Such a discussion will go a long way toward clarifying what you want to support.

ONE FAMILY FOUNDATION'S VALUES

A new foundation was holding a two-day retreat to come to agreement about how the family was to make this new endeavor work. I suggested that one of the first topics on the agenda should be to identify shared values for the foundation.

Using a set of values cards, the Charles D. Trover Family Foundation board members (Chuck and currently three of his four children) pinpointed these shared values:

- *Family*
- *Compassion*
- *Responsibility*
- *Competence*

These values will help the Trover Family Foundation shape its focus and the kinds of grants it will make in the future. Perhaps they'll fund efforts to strengthen the family unit, or training programs to build work skills.

Goal-Setting

I've asked new philanthropists more than a few times, "What are you trying to accomplish?" This is an important query to answer whenever you are giving money or property, whether as a checkbook philanthropist, a DAF donor, or the founder or trustee of a family foundation. Include in your answer your goals for the *act* of philanthropy, what *you* hope to experience by giving, as well as the *impact* of your philanthropy and what you hope to do for your community (however you define it) through your grantmaking.

Here are some examples:

For You, the Philanthropist

- I want my kids to be engaged in our community and feel compassion for those in need.
- I want the extended family to have something to do at Thanksgiving besides eat turkey.

- I want my husband and me to work with our children and grandchildren and undertake a thoughtful family project that we'll all enjoy together.
- I want my children to understand that to whom much is given, much is expected.
- My values are important to me and I want my children and grandchildren to understand why I think they're important.
- I'd like to know more about what my kids and grandkids care about and why.
- Learning more about what makes my community tick excites me, and I hope it will also excite my partner.

For Your Community

- I want to help reduce the number of people I see panhandling on the street.
- I believe that the arts are a great way to improve educational outcomes and want to bring them back to the schools.
- My kids have opportunities many others don't. I want others to have these chances as well.
- I think children thrive if adults pay attention to them. I'd like to make sure that all children have someone who cares and invests in them.
- Growing up I saw my best friend struggle with Crohn's disease. I think I could help fund the search for a cure for inflammatory bowel diseases.
- When I was a kid all the land around my town was wilderness. That's disappeared and become suburbs. I'd like to protect what wilderness is left for future generations.
- The entrepreneurial spirit can be taught. I'd like to support schools and organizations that help junior and high school students run small businesses.
- Racial and gender inequality still exist in the United States. I'd like to find ways to transform our society.

- I read that at least 16%[15] of inmates in jail nationwide are seriously mentally ill, as compared to 6% of all Americans.[16] Isn't there a better way to identify and treat mental illness when it first strikes?

You get the idea. You'll choose one or more of these goals or identify your own. Then you must answer the question, "How will I achieve them?" By sticking to your clearly defined values and goals, your grantmaking choices will more likely meet success.

Next, Figuring Out the Best Strategies

In your case, you're trying to determine how best you can achieve your goals. Regarding your personal or philanthropic practice goals, you're already taking a step by reading this book. Let's choose one of the community goals above and outline how you can identify strategies that will lead to good decisions. Since I'm writing the book and this is one of my interests, I've chosen the last one. How can you best help children cope with mental illness? How do you proceed?

1. Find out the scope of the problem. How many kids suffer from mental illness in your region?[17] Is there an advocacy organization near you (see National Alliance on Mental Illness)? Does your local school district have psychiatrist(s) who can give you an idea of the scope of the problem in schools? What about the local children's hospital? Estimates say that at least 20% of children and youth in the juvenile justice system suffer from serious mental illness, while up to 70% suffer mental health disorders.[18] Seek out local or state government agencies that could help inform you. For example, I just Googled® "Washington state mental health statistics

---

[15] E. Fuller Torrey, M.D., *et al.*, *More Mentally Ill Persons Are in Jails or Prisons Than Hospitals: A Survey of the State*, Treatment Advocacy Center and the National Sheriff's Association, May 2010.

[16] From http://www.nimh.nih.gov/health/publications/the-numbers-count-mental-disorders-in-america/index.shtml

[17] For example, nationally 4.6 million children received mental health services with a cost totaling $8.9 billion. This is from 2006 data from the U.S. Department of Health and Human Services, Agency for Healthcare Research and Quality's (AHRQ's) Medical Expenditure Panel Survey (MEPS) and a summary is available at the National Institute of Mental Health.

[18] Skowyra, Kathleen R. and Cocozza, PhD, Joseph J. *Blueprint for Change: A Comprehensive Model for the Identification and Treatment of Youth With Mental Health Needs in Contact with the Juvenile Justice System*, National Center for Mental Health and Juvenile Justice, with support from the Office of Juvenile Justice and Delinquency Prevention, U.S. Department of Justice, 2007.

children adolescents" and up came a 2007 report by the Washington State Office of Maternal and Child Health, *Children's Mental Health in Washington State: A public health perspective needs assessment.*

Don't forget that your fellow philanthropists can be good sources of information, too. Every foundation has its own goals and process. Some may delve more deeply than you plan to, and you can piggyback on strategies they've proven effective. Some might delve less deeply and go only by gut feel, but they may still be worth contacting. And reach out beyond those located nearby. Take a look at any directory of foundations (GuideStar and Foundation Center are two that are free with basic information as long as you register) and do a search for "mental health" and "children" and "adolescents" and see what foundations pop up. If they have a website, look them up. If not, call them. Just be prepared to carefully explain you are not seeking a grant but rather you are a trustee of a grantmaking foundation just starting to fund in the mental health arena and are looking for advice on best funding strategies. Ask if there is someone to speak to about this. A program officer? Executive director? Trustee? Your regional association of grantmakers can help you. I have always found other foundations, even those called, emailed, or otherwise contacted out of the blue, eager to assist philanthropic peers in their common efforts.

2. Discover the stumbling blocks to treatment. Take a look at the website of Effective Child Therapy: evidence based mental health for children and adolescents (http://www.effectivechildtherapy.com/). Talk to some of the psychiatrists you identified above. What is the ratio of child and adolescent psychiatrists to mentally ill children? What is the length of the waiting list to see one? (In Seattle, it's six months.) Is there hospital-based intensive treatment available in your community? How long does it take to get a bed when in crisis? Meet with the local university psychiatry and psychology department heads. See if your local National Association of Mental Illness chapter will put you in touch with families with mentally ill children and teens and talk with them about their experience. Or just ask around. I guarantee you'll find someone you know who's been addressing some of these issues.

3. Identify who is doing good work in this arena. Universities, hospitals, nonprofit clinics, schools or school systems, advocacy organizations, support groups, public health departments, and juvenile justice facilities are some of them. Ask each of them about the gaps in funding and services to children in need of mental health services. See if there is agreement on what is needed. Perhaps commission recommendations from them, or from university departments of social science, about what needs addressing to improve the field and even ask what they think X dollars could do to move the needle. Do you want to increase the number of kids being served? Reach out to help those with the most serious diagnoses? Work in conjunction with the juvenile justice system? Educate parents, teachers, and others in close contact with children and teens about symptoms of mental illness? Think about what makes sense to you.

4. Choose your decision-making criteria. This is where your values, goals, and strategies inform you. Deciding *how* you'll decide is an important step and one that, if not tackled with your board up front, can haunt you again and again in nasty disagreements, family arguments, and even a break-up of the foundation itself.

Are you interested in supporting work already being done that is evidence-based and proven? Replicating that proven program to additional organizations or locations? Identifying the best service provider and providing funding to increase its capacity to serve more people, more effectively? Give primarily to nonprofits with the financial wherewithal to be around next year (six months of operating funds in reserve, good financial oversight, and reporting systems and varied sources of support)? Provide a scholarship for child and adolescent physiatrists-in-training? Invest in new research or strategies? Concentrate on teenage suicide? Focus on an age group? Work within school systems?

Craft a form (Excel is fine)[19] using a 1 to 5 rating (or stars, or whatever works for you) for each question. Include other criteria you deem important: innovative, collaborative, compassionate, focuses on an underserved population, financial health, "I know the executive director and she's awesome," etc. All decision-makers can then use this form and you can, prior to or at a board meeting, compare each other's opinions and recommendations.

This exercise can help you eliminate some applications from discussion at the meeting, thus saving time. Even if your favorite proposal falls off the list by using this process, you can always choose to fund it through checkbook giving. Such a form is useful whether or not you

---

[19] There is grantmaking management system (GMS) software, cloud-based or otherwise, that will allow you track your decision-making processes and capture it within a database for easy retrieval and applicant communication.

accept unsolicited proposals. See the table above on this page (and continued on the next) for an example of what it could look like.

5. Learn from each grant. Think about the questions you'll think about and feel about your grant? Will you want to change your criteria or focus as a result?

In a nutshell, these steps will lead to a well-functioning, intentional, and rewarding philanthropy practice:

XYZ Foundation Criteria Rating Sheet (Scale of 0 to 5)											
Nonprofit Org Name	Fits Focus	Financial Status	Entrepreneurial Values	Leadership Strength	"Gut check"	Measure Results	Total	Average	Funded Previously?	Amount Requested	Comments:
A	4	2	2	3	3	2.5	16.5	2.8	N	$ 40,000.00	
B	5	4	4	3	5	4	25	4.2	N	$ 50,000.00	Really cool strategy!
C	3	4	2	5	3	2.5	19.5	3.3	N	$ 10,000.00	Like ED and board, but not exactly our focus
D	5	3.5	4	4	4	4	24.5	4.1	Y	$ 25,000.00	Across the board impressive
E	0						0	0.0	N	$ 5,000.00	Doesn't fit focus at all; didn't score.
F	5	3	5	4	5	3.5	25.5	4.3	Y	$ 15,000.00	This is the strongest application averages score, but I've questions about their financial strength.
G	4	3	2.5	3	3	1	16.5	2.8	Y	$ 20,000.00	How do they measure results?
H	4	3.5	2.75	3	4	3.5	20.75	3.5	N	$ 25,000.00	
I	4	2	3	2	1	0	12	2.0	N	$ 35,000.00	They've had 3 EDs in past year; leadership vacuum or mission blur?
J	2	5	5	4	3	2	21	3.5	N	$ 30,000.00	

First:

- Identify what you value.
- Set your goals.
- Determine your strategies.

Then:

- Scope out the problem.
- Find what stands in the way.
- Identify the exemplars.
- Agree on your decision-making criteria.
- Build your administrative infrastructure.

And finally:

- Learn from everything you do.

We've revisited values and goals and discussed grantmaking strategies. Now it's time to talk about administrative tools that can play an important part in how you effectively implement your strategies.

Administrative Challenges

Grant record keeping. You could use 3"x 5" cards to track your grantmaking process and history, but I don't recommend it. The first issue to consider is how many grants you will make annually. The more grants, the more a grantmaking management system (GMS) made specifically for these tasks will be helpful to you. For those who are interested in tracking grants made over time, keeping information about conversations with applicants and recipients, and looking back when the next application from them arrives, a GMS may be a necessity. It is also useful when evaluating your own activities.

They are expensive, however. The least expensive ones are in the range of $1,500 to $2,500 a year, but they are available at that price only if you are making very few grants. The next level is $3,000 to $5,000 a year, and $10,000 to $25,000 is more common. Large, complex foundations use GMS costing $100,000 annually. To determine if you want to invest in a GMS, ask yourself these questions:

- What kind of information do you want to track? For example, would you want to track the total number of grants you gave to arts organizations vs. education over the past three years?
- Do you want to accept applications online?
- How many people are involved in decision-making?
- Will you make a dozen or hundreds of grants in a year?
- Is the idea of clicking on a button to automatically send form letters and emails irresistibly appealing?

More than a dozen grantmaking management systems are available, and one should be right for you. Idealware ("helping nonprofits make smart software decisions" — see http://www.idealware.org) evaluates options. Its latest report, "Streamlining Online Grant Applications: A Review of Vendors," was published in 2010. Grants Managers Network (http://www.gmnetwork.org) can also be a good source of up-to-date information, and they were co-sponsors of this report which is available for download free on either website.

A simple database[20] that includes a "notes" field can serve you well, although over time, an Excel spreadsheet can get unwieldy. Combining this with form letters and mail merge, and a healthy dose of picking up the phone and talking, will keep you on top of your grantmaking.

Office space. Do you need it or will the kitchen drawer and table do? No and probably no. If you don't plan to employ in-house staff, there's no reason you must have an office. The kitchen drawer won't be large enough, but it is possible that your home office can be. If you do manage your foundation from your home, I suggest that you use a post office box for your address so that the foundation's contact information doesn't lead people directly to your home to drop off last minute applications. As anyone who works from home can attest, you may decide that a small off-site office is worth the investment if for no other reason than separating your personal from your philanthropic activities. Remember, though, that while you can count reasonable rent expense as part of the foundation's payout requirements, you cannot use that office for anything other than your foundation's work. I know a number of foundations with an office situated within, and the cost of the space donated by, the family business.

Staffing. The vast majority of family foundations don't have paid staff. Whether or not you need staffing is entirely dependent on your purpose and your desire to be hands-on with this work. If you accept unsolicited applications, you'll more likely need additional help unless your board is particularly large and likes to sort through what comes your way. If you use decision-making criteria that require in-depth review of an organization's financials, or you are particularly interested in helping nonprofits to measure progress toward their goals, then you may need some staff. Otherwise if you're small, don't accept unsolicited proposals, and enjoy the record keeping and proposal review processes, then you needn't hire staff, except perhaps for special projects. This isn't to say that you don't need an accountant and an attorney and, if you don't invest the foundation's corpus yourself, an investment adviser.

More times than I would have thought possible, I've run into donors or trustees who are groaning under the weight of a particular must-be-done-to-run-a-private-foundation task that they really, really hate. They may even have someone helping them with other needed tasks, but they keep the tasks they hate and outsource the ones they find rewarding. One

---

[20] There are databases stored on the cloud now available as well as software that even non-techies can set up and use with little or no help.

board was finding it difficult to rotate the responsibility of keeping minutes of its board meetings. Some were good at following through, others, for whatever reasons, weren't. A quick switch of responsibilities with part-time staff led to an arrangement with the staff person attending and writing up the board minutes, the trustees going on some site visits, and the board happier with its philanthropic activities. Remember, philanthropy *should* be fun.

Employee vs. consultant. What's the difference? Legal definitions apply here, and the IRS will be interested in whether you are meeting them. Basically we're talking about whether you want people who do what you tell them to or whether you are comfortable hiring a contractor to accomplish certain tasks.

Independent contractors must be in charge of their work space, tools and working hours and negotiate how they will accomplish the tasks you hire them to do. Consultants tend to have deep experience and can complete their job for you in less time than staff, but they also charge more because there will be fewer learned-on-the-job errors. There is also less paperwork because benefits such as medical insurance, retirement funding, etc., are included in the contractual rate that you pay rather than filed separately.

Full or part-time employees are different. You get to tell them exactly what to do and, if you so desire, how to do it. (Not that micromanaging is necessarily the best way to manage employees.) Employees usually have set work hours, undertake a variety of tasks from the menial to the complex, and are typically paid less than a consultant by the hour because you are also paying for their benefits (health insurance, half of social security and Medicare, retirement, unemployment insurance). You have to withhold these taxes and run payroll and issue a W-2 form with employees.

Employees may come with less experience than consultants. And don't forget: You must supervise, evaluate, and say nice things and potentially not nice things to employees. You may even need to fire someone who isn't working out. So make sure you check out all the relevant human resources issues with your lawyer before you hire someone.

At times you may need both consultants and employees. A consultant can set up a system for current or future employees to use and modify, or be called in to perform specialized research, application review and analysis, or facilitation gigs that the employee either hasn't the time or the skills to undertake.

Hiring someone you know. With small and start-up family foundations, it's more likely that a lucky connection, rather than someone's level of experience, results in their being hired as an employee. Why is this? Because we're talking about money. Money can be a sensitive issue to people who have it (and people who don't, for that matter) and trust can be a more important issue to you than expertise. As a result, you'll often find small family foundations hiring a friend, neighbor, clergy member, accountant, attorney, or other family member. Is this a good thing? It is true that relatively smart people can learn the art and science of grantmaking, and if you feel comfortable with this option, you may decide to go for it. Whoever you hire will go through a steep learning curve. If they come to it without grantmaking experience, send them to conferences, find them a mentor, or hire a coach to help them get comfortable with their role.

Hiring someone with experience. If you decide you want to bring in someone with more grantmaking know-how, I can assure you that you will have more than enough incredibly qualified people applying for the post. There are two ways to do this: yourself, by hiring someone, or using a firm to conduct a professional search. One leads to lots of applications coming your way that you must sort, acknowledge, check references, and interview. The second path leads to lots of applications going to the search firm that sorts, checks references, and recommends the top candidates to interview. Be careful, though. Make sure the search consultant or firm understands family foundations. It isn't enough to be experienced in the charitable not-for-profit sector because family foundations are different beasts. The search firm also may have someone already in its files that it may "push" without regard to your needs. The person you hire needs to be sensitive to your and your family's feelings about the foundation, represent the foundation within the community, and recognize that he or she has some, but possibly not much, involvement in the decisions made.

Nonetheless, search firms and consultants have connections with people who already do this kind of work and can cut short the search time and potentially produce a better fit. Don't forget that thinking through the job description, especially the skills and characteristics of the person you want in your office, will also be important. After all, this *is* sensitive work, both in how the employee works with you and with the applying nonprofit charities.

If you do decide to look for candidates yourself, use your own connections and networks, plus post jobs on your local regional association of grantmakers website (http://www.givingforum.org). If you're interested in expanding your search, several online national job banks that specialize in nonprofit work can help you. These include Opportunity Knocks, Idealist.org, Young Nonprofit Professionals Network — find the chapter near you — and Encore, which specializes in helping people embarking on second careers find jobs in the nonprofit sector. There are also grantmaking-specific national job lists such as Philanthropy Careers in the *Chronicle of Philanthropy* (http://www.philanthropy.com), the Council on Foundations, and Future Leaders in Philanthropy (FLIP).

The national firms that specialize in finding staff for grantmaking foundations tend to seek executive directors or very senior program officers, usually for large foundations. The cost? A third of the annual salary being offered is typical, although I've conducted searches on an hourly basis. Still others may charge up to a year's salary. I'll let you Google® search firms, since there are several. *The Chronicle of Philanthropy* has published a number of articles about foundations using search firms.

Setting your employees' salaries. Most large metropolitan regions have salary surveys — either of the nonprofit sector (check your local United Way, nonprofit association or community foundation) or sometimes even for private foundations (check your local regional association of grantmakers). Paying a reasonable wage is a good thing, but if you've hired one of your family members, you'll need to document, using appropriate comparisons, that you're not self-dealing by paying that granddaughter an unreasonably high salary. This, in particular, is why a salary survey is useful. Otherwise, think about the job itself and compare those responsibilities to similar for-profit positions to set the wage. Small foundations that hire part-time employees should take into consideration that there is little chance for an employee to move up in the foundation's hierarchy, so make sure the person you hire is comfortable with this and is compensated at a level that keeps him or her happy.

Consultants set their fees based either on the job ($XX a month for serving as a *de facto* program officer), or by the hour. Some consultants set their fees high because they believe they offer the best service and have the most experience. Others set their fees at a point where they believe they've hit a sweet spot for offering good value for the price. And of course there are some who are just starting out as consultants and are trying to undercut the market to gain their first clients.

Finding colleagues to help. In common with most industries, philanthropy has a support infrastructure. There are dozens of organizations and associations of grantmakers that can aid and inform you in your endeavors.

National membership associations such as the Council on Foundations, Association for Small Foundations (http://www.smallfoundations.org), National Committee for Responsive Philanthropy (progressive), and The Philanthropy Roundtable (conservative) address philanthropy broadly.

Regional associations of grantmakers allow members to mingle regularly, build peer networks, learn from conferences and workshops, and collaborate with funders in your own region. See the Forum of Regional Associations of Grantmakers (http://www.givingforum.org) to find the regional association near you.

Affinity groups of grantmakers concerned with specific issues (e.g., Grantmakers in Health), or function (e.g., Emerging Practitioners in Philanthropy for those new to the field), or that share a perspective or ethnicity (e.g., Association of Black Foundation Executives), are also available to you. For a pretty complete list see the Council on Foundations' affinity group list (http://www.cof.org/about/affinitygroups.cfm).

There are also academic and study centers that study the nonprofit sector or grantmaking such as the Independent Sector, the Johnson Center for Philanthropy at Grand Valley State University, Harvard University's Hauser Center, New York University's School of Law's National Center for Philanthropy and the Law, and the Indiana University Lilly Family School of Philanthropy.

The National Center for Family Philanthropy is an independent, nonprofit national center committed to developing resources and support for donors, their families, staff and advisors and is worth a special look by family foundation donors, board members and staff.

Groups with specific teaching to improve the nonprofit sector are helpful as well. After all, if your job is to provide funding to nonprofits to achieve shared goals, you want the nonprofits to have access to helpful resources. See BoardSource (https://boardsource.org/eweb), National

Council for Nonprofit Associations
(http://www.councilofnonprofits.org) and the newsletter *Blue Avocado*
(http://www.blueavocado.org) with the ever-wonderful nonprofit
executive director and blogger Vu Le
(http://www.nonprofitwithballs.com).

This is by no means a complete list of the resources available to you.
However, I encourage you to take advantage of them. They offer
research, learning from peers, opportunities to talk about the issues you
care about with others who share your interest, workshops, webinars, and
conferences.

Are you scared to death now? Does it sound too complicated? It *is*
complicated. But thinking through these issues before you start
grantmaking will make it all much easier in the long run. Now let's go into
more detail about some of the steps that will make operating a family
foundation even easier, more enjoyable, and likely to accomplish your
goals.

6 | FINDING YOUR FOCUS

There are few hard and fast rules about a foundation's grantmaking procedures; regulatory bodies that oversee the field tend to be limited to the IRS, your state's Attorney General and Congress. The only way you'll know you're accomplishing *something* is if you first decide *what* you're trying to accomplish with your grantmaking.

One way to make it easier is to choose a focus. Most people are generally seeking to do some kind of good or enable some kind of change. I've touched on this before, but let's briefly review.

What issue or cause tugs at your heartstrings? What keeps you awake at night? Or excites you so that you jump up and down and smile?

- Are children the love of your life?
- Do the arts move you to tears?
- Does injustice make you angry?
- Is entrepreneurial success something you have experienced and want to share?
- Are you a sports fanatic?
- Is the wilderness where you recharge?
- Do you believe that a high quality education is the most important step toward a successful life?

Most people have *something* that's at the top of their list of passions. Let's say you love both community theatre and helping people in poverty climb out. You can focus on both these issues. Or fund community theatre that performs inspirational plays with a social justice, anti-poverty bent.

Many funders don't want to limit themselves. They are interested in all issues: arts, education, health, environment, community development, etc. Funding the whole kit and caboodle is possible and commonly described in private foundations' articles of incorporation and bylaws. Funding in all issue areas opens all doors. This is okay, but it makes it potentially more time-consuming and more difficult to choose the best options to support.

Sometimes donors will identify their values and choose to fund nonprofits in any focus area that shares those values. A typical value might be helping people to help themselves. Or to encourage collaborative efforts between multiple organizations. Or to help promising nonprofits to build their capacity to achieve their missions. I've known a few foundations that rotate issues they support each or every other year; many just decide they wish to fund what they discover each year no matter what issue that may be.

It is fairly obvious that the less focused you are, the less able you are to achieve your goals, because you won't know what they are, and the less able you will be to evaluate either your grantees' or your own successes. If you are primarily attempting to practice philanthropy as a family endeavor rather than making change happen in your community, then this may be less of an issue for you.

Another way to consider which issues are most important to you is to review your past charitable gifts. Take a look at the last three years of your tax returns where you list your donations. Categorize them. Think about where most of your donations have gone. You may be surprised at what comes out on top. Were they intentional choices? Or were they casual decisions because friends asked you to support *their* favorite causes, or a neighbor came to your door collecting? Not that these are bad choices, but do you have a history of giving to what *you* want to support?

Even if you're coming to this book already experienced with a family foundation, reviewing past grants can surprise you. I had a client whose trustees were sure their foundation was an "education" grantmaker. After analyzing the previous five years of giving, it become obvious that it was more of a social services grantmaker. Again, both are fine focus areas. But being intentional about what you do will allow you to figure out if you're actually doing it.

Clarity of focus eases the process of reviewing applications or requesting proposals and finally determining where your grants will go. Such clarity also makes it easier to "tell your story" (discussed in Chapter 11), assess whether you're going the right direction, and determine why and how to say "no." (Saying no is a part of grantmaking that no one has yet figured out how to make easy, although I'll give you a clue later.) The Laird Norton Family Foundation story above also provides insight into another factor that will help make grant decisions easier: your geographical focus. And that is the subject of the next chapter.

CRAFTING A FOCUS

Watershed protection had been a focus area for the 8th generation Laird Norton Family Foundation for many years. The family wealth came originally from the sale of timber. After a liquidity event that grew the foundation's size, family members involved wanted to revisit that focus area and see if they could be more effective in their giving. They invited nonprofit leaders and other experts to provide ideas — in writing and in discussions — about how the foundation could support watershed stewardship in the Pacific Northwest and actually see progress over time. It resulted in the identification of several watersheds (vs. all watersheds in the Pacific Northwest) in which to concentrate through a set of criteria including:

- *Ecological significance*
- *Partnerships between on-the-ground organizations*
- *Community engagement and support*
- *Supportive governmental regulations or watershed improvement plans*
- *Ongoing scientific monitoring*
- *The presence and activities of other funders*

All of the Laird Norton Family Foundation's grants are now rated against this set of criteria, which is possible because the family honed its focus to something that could be measured, was informed by experts, and connected to its values. See http://www.lairdnorton.org for more information.

7 | WHERE IN THE WORLD SHOULD YOU FUND?

Think about where you have made your donations until now. Are they typically near where you live? Or where you went to university? Or where you grew up? Perhaps there are national organizations serving causes you care about. Or maybe you took that trip to a lesser-developed country (LDC) and were moved by what you saw and decided to try to make a difference there. There are reasons to choose one or all of these "places." Let's explore them further.

Private foundations tend to call the region(s) they fund their "geographic focus." This can be an oxymoron because if you fund in a variety of regions, there's not really a focus, is there? But many foundations decide to define their geographic giving areas as a way to limit the number of proposals they receive (if they accept and consider all applications) or to draw some other limit so that their grantmaking is relevant to them personally and not overwhelming in terms of the number of nonprofits that potentially could receive their largesse. Sometimes, grantmakers want to visit their grantees — and it is much easier to do so in a region rather than in the nation or the entire world. Again, it can be helpful to think about what you're trying to accomplish as a way to guide your decision about where you make grants.

Limiting Your Grantmaking to a Specific Geographic Place

There are foundations that have made the decision to concentrate on what is called "place-based grantmaking" not just because they happen to be located in that place but because they believe that concentrating their efforts on an issue *in one place* provides a greater chance of success. There are several definitions of this phrase, and indeed, additional terms used to think about place-based giving: "embedded funders" and "grassroots grantmakers" are two. I like the following definition by Grassroots Grantmakers executive director Janis Foster Richardson:

> A place-based funder has an intimate tie to a particular place that you can find on a map, and is focusing their work in that place with the people who live there and the organizations and institutions that are highly invested in that place. A place-base funder uses a wide-angle, multi-faceted lens in work that is about community resilience and vitality. They may work on one problem or issue at a time, but do so with respect for local history and culture, a commitment to identifying and mobilizing local assets, and an interest in building local capacity to weather the next storm.[21]

One foundation that practices this type of philanthropy (anonymously quoted in a report) described it as:

> …immersing yourself in the community. You get the best information you can, based on what the people tell you and what you see…And then you stay. You stay and humble yourself every day and you listen.[22]

In general, place-based grantmaking means being committed to a neighborhood or community and for the long term, truly listening to the community identify its own needs, and helping to build capacity to attain them. Those who take it the furthest are grantmakers who actually place their office in the neighborhood they fund and consistently seek out advice from their potential grant recipients and other community leaders. It's pretty hard to be a place-based grantmaker without either staff who are engaged in the community or a board willing to spend the time themselves in that endeavor.

---

[21] From *Big Thinking on Small Grants*, posted August 27, 2009,
http://janisfoster.blogspot.com/2009/08/wanting-more-from-place-based.html.
[22] "Moving Forward While Staying in Place: Embedded Funders and Community Change," Chapin Hall Discussion Paper, Chapin Hall, Center for Children, University of Chicago, October, 2004.

Note that community foundations often operate as place-based funders, and if you have decided on a DAF, you can take advantage of their expertise to help you follow place-based funders' principles.

Legacy Grantmaking

Another popular term in philanthropy is "legacy." "I want to leave a legacy" to honor my parents, my former employees, my customers.

Legacy grantmaking can be as simple as ensuring that gifts are given in the town or city where the money was earned. Or at the summer home where the family traditionally relaxed. It can also be a special grant program focusing on an issue or place that was close to the donor's heart. Some family foundations, usually in succeeding generations, have moved their place of operations or changed their focus areas, but they still want to honor their donors and their donors' intent. One way to do so is to budget for a special grant, perhaps a large one, made in memory of their ancestors, where they lived, and concerning an issue they cared about.

Nationwide Grantmaking

Some foundations, — especially second, third, and later generation family foundations — make grants wherever family members reside. With multiple generations, this can make for an interesting grant map. It can be very useful and rewarding to the next generation(s) to be able to recommend grants in the towns where they now live and not be limited to making gifts in the town where they grew up. This generational diaspora does cause stress on a foundation that often limits its grantmaking to the hometown region.

Giving Internationally:
Does It Accomplish More?

Yes and no. Certainly LDCs have standards of living that tend to allow U.S. dollars to go further. And you could probably afford to adopt a village in, say, Haiti, and send all children in that village to school, if that's what you want to do.

(Providing help after a natural disaster is a somewhat different story. There are lots of lessons learned about what works best and what fails. See the Center for Disaster Philanthropy (http://disasterphilanthropy.org/when/principles-of-disaster-management/disaster-grantmaking/) for a guide to effective disaster relief funding. Its first principle: "Do no harm.")

But there are many complications that can enter the picture, and you should be aware of them if you want to give internationally. First of all, you must not underestimate the cultural — as well as economic, language, religious, and other — differences between where you grew up and reside in North America and any other country. For instance, countries where bribes are just part of the system (no judgment) tend to lessen the buying power of your dollars.

Second, you are many thousands of miles away from where your grant money is being invested. Site visit to Columbia, anyone? Who will be ensuring that the organization that gets your dollars is accomplishing what you hope to accomplish?

Private foundations are required to give their money to entities that serve the public good. In the United States, public charities have "proof" of that by the IRS tax determination letter most are awarded (with some exceptions, notably places of worship), documenting their section 501(c)(3) charitable status. Most LDCs haven't a governmental system that polices their non-governmental organizations (NGOs) to ensure no one is running off with the goods. To prove to our IRS that your gift is charitable, you will have to use a process called "exercising expenditure responsibility." This entails extra recordkeeping that demonstrates that you investigated the organization thoroughly to verify its charitable purposes, and reviewed its financials to confirm that your grant dollars were appropriately spent (the grant recipient must keep a separate account for those funds, as well). Alternately, you may request the IRS make an equivalency determination about the specific NGO. This takes time and dollars on your part, but if you intend to continue supporting the organization, this determination will allow you to do the regular amount of due diligence vs. the extra expenditure responsibility for future grants. And in this post-9/11 era, you also need to demonstrate appropriate procedures to avoid, even unwittingly, funding terrorism.

Lastly, learn from the legendary number of well-meaning but ultimately abandoned or failed international projects. The last thing you be is the "ugly American" stereotype.

LEARNING ABOUT FAILURE

If you take the time to speak with others who have funded internationally, I guarantee you'll learn some amazing and heartening stories of how their donations have helped save lives — as well as also tales of how few were helped or how the well broke and then was never fixed when funds were provided for repairs. Or worse, how your money lined the pockets of a corrupt individual or group. Two good sources of these lessons are Engineers Without Borders Failure Reports (http://legacy.ewb.ca/en/whoweare/accountable/failure.html), which annually reports on such mistakes and what was learned from them; and Admitting Failure (http://www.admittingfailure.com/about/), a website that invites people to share their failings within civil society organizations.

There are many organizations and experienced people who can help make your international grantmaking more meaningful. Or you can decide to make all grants to U.S.-based "Friends of" 501(c)(3) public charities that operate independently of the foreign organization but raise money to support their efforts. With this approach, you don't have to exercise expenditure responsibility or conduct the extra record keeping that the IRS requires when you grant to an organization that isn't a 501(c)(3) or proven to be its equivalent. There are also intermediaries such as the Charities Aid Foundation, Give2Asia, or the King Baudouin Foundation that will make it simpler for you to send your money abroad. But don't expect that giving internationally is *easier* because your dollars have more purchase power. Rewarding it can be, but it will also be full of potholes.

Just so you know, there are affinity groups (NGO Source and African Grantmakers Network, for example) and giving circles with an international focus (Pangea: Giving for Global Change) through which you can learn more about international giving, its difficulties, and rewards. And there are remarkable nonprofits with deep experience working internationally. Talk with several of them if you can. Google® Peter Blomquist's TedxRainier Talk given in Seattle in 2011.

And there are new organizations that are making interesting claims that small direct gifts to the poor create more change than other, more traditional, international aid methodologies. Take a look at Give Directly (http://www.givedirectly.org), which encourages people to give through them to provide $500 a year for two years directly (through cell phones) to the poorest families in a region in Kenya to spend however they want. They find the poorest (on average living on 65 cents a day) simply by giving only to people who live in mud huts with thatched roofs. Give Directly has partnered with groups that are undertaking rigorous evaluations that will soon be available.

Once you decide to make your grants throughout your city, county, state or region, you start to deal with issues of scale. How can you find and evaluate the best choices when you have opened your geographic area so widely that the numbers of potential grant recipients — or if you're accepting proposals, applications — becomes quite large?

Here again, it is important to understand and accept the fact that decision-making in philanthropy is not likely to be entirely objective. You may have proposals from two hospitals seeking help to provide better care for the frail elderly. You might think you can evaluate each proposal and decide that Hospital "A" has a better idea or track record or will serve more people than Hospital "B." And you may be able to. But if you're not an expert with experience in hospital service delivery, your evaluation may be missing some piece of information that could have caused you to choose differently. It's also possible that there are other hospitals in your city that already provide the same services or have a better idea. Or a community clinic with better outreach to the frail elderly could be a more effective location from which to supply such services.

So remember, as much as you hope you are being objective, realize that some subjectivity comes into every decision, based on the information at hand, the ability (or inability) of the applicant to tell its story, and simply who's in the room (e.g., who has applied for a grant or what problem has come to light in the media).

If you are granting in several areas or a wide range of issues in your geographic community, it can become a bit overwhelming to learn about all of the nonprofits in various places, review unsolicited applications, and become an expert in strategies that have been successful.

If you're unable, for whatever reason, to do the homework, think closely about why you want to give in an extensive region, such as statewide. Is it because you love that local museum near where you visit each summer and want to support it as well as the symphony in your city on the other side of the state? You may want to consider limiting your giving to your city and that over-the-mountain town. Otherwise applicants might get their hopes up when they see "Washington State" when you really mean "Seattle" *and* "Twisp, WA." Maybe you just want to be free to fund wherever you run into something worth supporting. Of course, if you don't accept unsolicited proposals, then it isn't necessary to limit your funding's geographic reach to make it more manageable.

8 | TYPES OF GRANTS YOU CAN MAKE

We've discussed how selecting a focus and determining where you'll make grants will ease your grantmaking process. Here is another topic to assist you: What kinds of grants do you want to make?

I can hear those new to grantmaking wonder what the heck I'm talking about. "Grants," you say, "It's a check. Given to a nonprofit."

Yes, it is, but the check can be for a purpose that is as broad as "for whatever the nonprofit needs" to as specific as to pay "for a Intuit QuickBooks nonprofit financial software package and training for the nonprofit's bookkeeper."

Here are many of the types of grants you can make.

General Operating:
Keeping the Lights On

An "operating" or "general operating" grant is one that supports the nonprofit as a whole. There are foundations that give only general operating grants because they decide that, after identifying a high quality nonprofit they wish to support, they might as well provide funding that the nonprofit can apply to whatever it needs most. Personally, I believe this is an immensely sensible choice. But some grantmakers don't like funding general operating because they believe the money may sink into a big hole, or increase the executive director's salary beyond what is appropriate. They may be concerned that they can't track the effect of their grant. For decades the question of whether to provide general operating support was hotly debated.

But during the past decade or so, that question has largely been laid to rest.[23] General support can be effective. But there are still funders who would rather fund something they can see, touch, put their name on, or identify with. A new program is exciting. So is providing funding to expand or replicate something that works. Seeing the building or the van driving around town with your grantee's name on it (and maybe even your foundation's) can bring a sense of pride to many donors. Paying for toilet paper or salaries or the electric bill can seem much less exciting or rewarding.

I think general operating support is a good choice for several reasons:
1. Nonprofits have to pay for utilities and other mundane costs just like any other business, organization or homeowner.
2. The largest items in most nonprofits' budget are salaries and benefits but without staff, nothing will get done.
3. If you trust the nonprofit enough to give them a grant for a project or a building, why not help the organization as a whole in support of its mission?
4. Cash flow is a challenge for most nonprofits, especially when you consider that government grants are usually paid late, donors give more at the end of the year (which may not coincide with the nonprofit's fiscal year), and foundations all have differing deadlines.
5. Operating support is the most flexible funding a nonprofit can have, leading to innovation, the ability to take advantage of strategic opportunities, and strengthening nonprofits as a whole.
6. General operating support is the most difficult for nonprofits to raise. As a result, you will be mightily loved.

---

[23] While the argument has gone on for many decades, I credit Paul Brainerd (founder and CEO of Aldus PageMaker which, when sold to Adobe, funded Brainerd's philanthropy) and his colleagues who started Social Venture Partners — a move I believe proved that general operating support is a worthy choice for grantmakers. SVP gives only general operating and has consistently studied, evaluated and shared their results with others.

Capacity Building:
Training, Equipment and R & D

Instead of general operating, some funders decide to provide money specifically to build a nonprofit's capacity to achieve its mission. Others will argue that this is exactly what general operating support does. It's an interesting debate.

Think of what could help a nonprofit do what it does better and "sustain itself over time."[24]

- Well-trained staff and leadership
- Excellence in communications
- Technology that is up to date
- Fundraising expertise
- A sabbatical for an exhausted CEO (see box, next page)
- Succession preparation
- Merger or reconstruction planning
- Savvy collaboration
- A game plan for the future

All of these are vital for a healthy nonprofit. You can pay for a consultant or coach, cover annual salary and benefits for a development director or chief operating officer,[25] purchase software and pay for training to use it, support conference registration for staff, or finance board training and resources (buy guides for each board member from BoardSource, for example). To determine what types of capacity building support your applicant can best use, ask them.

For a description of one family foundation's determination to build nonprofit capacity, read the Campion Foundation's "Charting Impact Report: Capacity Building."[26]

---

[24] Definition from the National Council on Nonprofits, http://www.councilofnonprofits.org/public-policy/federal-issues/nonprofit-capacity-building.

[25] For smaller nonprofits think of these as a "fundraiser" and "assistant director."

[26] See http://www.campionfoundation.org/downloads/capacity-building-strategy-2012.pdf

> ### AN UNUSUAL CAPACITY BUILDING GRANT
>
> *After a dozen years leading a nonprofit association, the executive director experienced a family crisis: her 7-year-old son suddenly developed symptoms of a mental illness. Thanks to one particular board member who underwrote the cost, her board of directors graciously provided her a paid leave of absence. As a result, that 7-year old was quickly treated by doctors and supported by family in an intensive manner that allowed for a complete recovery. That executive director was me; the board was the board of directors of Philanthropy Northwest; and the funder was a member of that board and president of a family foundation. Eventually, this act allowed for a transition to the next generation of leadership for Philanthropy Northwest …and me writing this book.*

Project/Program Support:
Increasing the Number Served,
Improving the Service Provided

This is probably the most common type of grant. You learn about a nonprofit that is providing an interesting service and you want to help it grow. Or one that is innovative and new and it strikes you as worth support. You can point to the YWCA's program to help older unemployed women to find and keep new jobs and say, "I helped do that." Since, for example, the Seattle-King County YWCA has nearly 50 distinct programs (under categories including housing, emergency help, employment, health and youth), by funding a particular one of them you can more easily explain what your dollars are intended for.

If you fund programs and projects, be aware of one potential risk: You may be wagging the tail of the dog. In other words you may be determining what programs the nonprofit should prioritize. Often applicants will look at a foundation's past funding, see what types of programs they tend to support, and decide to describe something they already do in a manner that makes it seem similar. Other times they may even take on a project that a funder wants, which makes the "grant" more like a "contract."[27] Sometimes those projects are suggested directly by the

---

[27] You may need to take care here; foundations that require a grant recipient to sign a grant agreement can cause their grantees to land in a pickle, as those in Washington State did in the 1980s. The state's Department of Revenue decided that anything that looked or even smelled like a contract — even merely requiring a reporting back of the results of the funding — was "a fee for service" and tried to tax nonprofits on their contracted "fees." The nonprofit and grantmaking community managed to get the regulations changed, but in this era of government

funder as something they'll support, and the nonprofit will decide that it will help pay for some existing salaries, even if those workers have to take on additional work.

A nonprofit providing services may wish to first perfect its programming by keeping its client base manageable rather than increasing the number it serves before it is ready. Listen to the nonprofit and let it identify its priorities. Don't be afraid to make suggestions, but allow it to give you reasons why that is either a good — or a bad — idea at this point in time.

Seed/Start-Up Funding:
The Joys and Downsides of Risk-taking

I said before that general operating support is difficult for nonprofits to acquire. Start-up or seed funding can be even more of a challenge. That's probably a good thing, though. If you run into people who are seeking money to start a nonprofit — and, as a philanthropist, you will — it's a good time to ask, "Who else is doing anything similar to what you're trying to accomplish?" If they don't know, suggest that funding from you won't be in the cards until they learn the answer to this question. If they do know what else is going on but can describe how their approach is somehow different or how it serves a neglected clientele, still suggest they consider ways to collaborate.

Could they find a fiscal sponsor rather than create a brand new nonprofit? A fiscal sponsor is an entity with the same general mission of a project idea whose board agrees to accept the program or project as one of its own. All funds raised are technically the fiscal sponsor's, and it is entitled to keep all the money. Usually a percentage of the income is retained to cover its expenses of bookkeeping, time, and even staffing, if shared. Note that there are good reasons not to use a fiscal sponsor. The visionary may not wish to give up his or her autonomy to do what they want to do; there may be philosophical or cultural reasons why the obvious fiscal sponsor choice won't work; or it might not be possible to find a fiscal sponsor.[28]

---

budget cutting, you never know. Check with your attorney, but I suggest using language that doesn't approach or use the word "contract."

[28] Perhaps you might invest in a few copies of Greg Colvin's book, *Fiscal Sponsorship, 6 Ways to Do It Right*, (Study Press Center, 2006), and hand them out when someone knocks on your door to ask about starting a nonprofit.

Then there are new ideas that you think are what my grandmother might have called the "bee's knees." (For those born after the 1960s, that means, "cool", according to the *Urban Dictionary*.) And you *want* to be in on the ground floor of getting it going. Start-up or seed funding may be appropriate here, but you should either provide multi-year funding, and enough to get over the hurdles of starting-up,[29] or matching dollars to bring in other funders to support the endeavor. There are other options, and it can become complicated.

How comfortable you are with risk, whether for start-up funding or for any kind of project or organization, is something that you should gauge beforehand. Remember, we learn from failures, and many foundations set aside a portion of their portfolio for risky endeavors. It is one of the delights of private donations — if you allow it, such spending can be the nonprofit sector's R & D money.

Capital Giving: Bricks and Mortar

Some people love being able to actually touch their gift. A brick in the ground. A van to deliver people to a service (kids to a Boys and Girls Club) or a service to people (Meals on Wheels). A phone system. Medical equipment. The education room in a museum. The wing of a hospital. An entire building. Some funders provide only this type of support.

The challenges here are that as the gift gets bigger (you're talking millions of dollars if you're into helping with the erection of a wing or building), you need to become expert in construction, property evaluation, financial statements and *pro formas*, etc. You may already have this expertise because of your line of business. If so, great. Then this is something you can take on confidently. Otherwise, you want to make sure that if you are paying for part of something, the other parts are also paid for or at least in sight before you release the funds. You can make a conditional grant ("We'll provide X dollars when you've achieved Y dollars in pledges") or even a below-market loan where the plan is that

---

[29] Let me introduce you to an IRS concept called "tipping." If you provide most or all of the funding to run a nonprofit, it may cause the organization to fail a public support test that likely forms the basis for its public charity status. They can be "tipped" into becoming a 501(c)(3) private foundation which makes them subject to the 5% payout rate, a 2% tax on net investment income, excise tax if they fail to meet various regulations, restrictive investment rules, and a less favorable tax deduction for their donors. This would be rather disastrous for the nonprofit, although there are grants that can be labeled "unusual grants" that may help avoid this problem. See your attorney (and have the nonprofit talk to their's, too).

you'll see that money returned over time and you can re-use it to make additional grants. (See program-related investments below, under Loans.)

Note that for large capital gifts you'll be asking for different kinds of information than for small ones or for other types of grants. Capital gifts also offer opportunities for you to name something concrete after your family, your donor, or your foundation.

Naming Opportunities: In Honor of...

Some people believe in "naming gifts" and others think they're too ostentatious. (See below for the pros and cons of giving anonymously.) But for those who do, your foundation's name on a plaque or on a building can serve a good purpose.

Your name on a nonprofit's van or room (or even just in its annual report as a funder) loudly proclaims: "This nonprofit is worthy of support." Others are influenced when they hear of a foundation they know and trust offering money to a nonprofit. That nonprofit may receive additional needed funds from those others, as a result. This is a good thing. Another reason to consider naming opportunities is to influence your children.

NAMING GIFTS AFFECT THE NEXT GENERATION OF DONORS

"When I see my family's name on things, I mostly feel proud and also an obligation to continue philanthropy in my generation," said the grandchild of the donor of a foundation in a next-generation meeting I helped facilitate. She may have felt conspicuous as a teenager, but as a young adult, she appreciates the lessons such naming opportunities have taught her.

Giving Anonymously

Some people decide not to allow their name to be posted on a wall because of religious reasons. Others are merely modest. Some are concerned about their children's safety (especially young ones). And still others just want to save the nonprofit the cost and effort of putting up a plaque.

Of course, if you are giving through a private foundation your grant is public information available to all by law (although your attorney will have some ways up their sleeve to provide donor anonymity). If you want to give anonymously on a regular basis, you may want to re-visit your philanthropy vehicle choice. A grant made through a donor advised fund, a grantor trust or single-member LLC might serve you better in this situation.

Multi-Year Giving

Multi-year giving to nonprofits you support is indicative of a very strong relationship between a funder and a nonprofit and its mission. It's one of the quirks of philanthropy that those foundations that do make multi-year grants usually put a limit on the number of years they will do so, often three to five years. Then the nonprofit cannot apply for a grant again for some period of time, often a year. The reason behind this is so that the foundation can distribute its limited resources over a wider variety of worthy beneficiaries, including those founded recently. There are always more applicants than a foundation can fund, and many are as worthy as another. Another reason, less often publicly voiced, is that foundation trustees may find it boring to fund the same organization repeatedly and want to move on to something new and different.

In some ways, denying a nonprofit multi-year funding or limiting that funding to a certain number of years is kind of like punishing them for success. You wouldn't be providing such a level of support if you didn't think what the nonprofit was doing was successful. Or deserving of a lift to the next level. But foundations often express the fear that nonprofits will become dependent upon them and use this as a reason not to provide multi-year funding. Hey, nonprofit leaders are adults. They'll hope for continued funding, but if warned, they'll be grown-up about not getting it.

A few foundations decide that long-term funding is so important that when they find the right nonprofit, they decide to provide 10-year support or on-going support until something occurs that changes their direction. A nonprofit CEO who actually knows when the next financial influx is coming can concentrate on process, progress, evaluation and innovation, rather than primarily on fundraising.

But resources are finite. So what do you do? You could choose as few as one or two nonprofits annually for a multi-year grant. Perhaps choose one that is eligible only if you've supported it previously, and you put it in the running yourself by invitation. Or you could provide a multi-year grant to only one organization at a time. This approach would both preserve your assets as well as reward good work in at least some cases.

Or you can decide that multi-year gifts are fine; they support excellent organizations and allow you to know your donations are well placed. And they cut back on the number of organizations you might invite to apply since you know your budget into the near future is limited to dollars that aren't already committed.

Loans

Yes, you can make loans or equity investments to support public charities. Program-Related Investments (PRIs) are below-market rate investments that are eligible to count against the 5% payout private foundations are required to make each year in the tax law. However, when the loan is repaid, it increases your foundation's required distribution so it must be "redeployed" to keep the benefit of counting toward the 5% payout requirement. The Internal Revenue Code describes PRIs in this way:

- An investment, the primary purpose is to accomplish one or more of the foundation's exempt purposes.
- Production of income or appreciation of property is not a significant purpose.
- Influencing legislation or taking part in political campaigns on behalf of candidates is not a purpose.[30]

According to Mission Investors Exchange, an association of grantmakers interested in making loans and other mission-related investments, "PRIs may be made in the form of loans, loan guarantees, cash deposits, equity investments and other investments made for a specific purpose such as affordable workforce housing and community development facilities. Foundations…may include PRIs as part of their grant budget, or choose to view PRIs within the context of their endowment investment allocation."[31]

Foundations can benefit from PRIs as a way to keep a rotating fund available for charitable investment, one that counts toward their payout, and keeps their asset value from declining. PRIs require that you conduct

---

[30] http://www.irs.gov/Charities-&-Non-Profits/Private-Foundations/Program-Related-Investments
[31] https://www.missioninvestors.org/mission-investing

significant due diligence and oversight and generally require legal involvement, but there are many resources to help.

Among the various instruments you can use in a PRI are common loans, certificates of deposit in a community development bank, linked deposits, and common stock, preferred stock, and loan guarantees.[32]

Mission-Related Investments

Mission-related investments (MRIs) are another method a foundation can use to make progress towards its mission. Mission-related investing is similar to PRIs as both are mission-driven investment opportunities. However, while PRIs must earn only below-market rates of return (and are therefore seen as a program more than an investment), MRIs are true investments that seek market rate returns and do not count against the 5% payout requirement. For example, a foundation concerned about low-income housing may choose to invest in a real estate development project that includes a greater share of low-income units than is typical. MRI opportunities exist across asset classes in cash, fixed income, public equity, private equity, venture capital, and real estate.

You'll probably end up making many kinds of these grants, loans and investments. Some foundations decide that concentrating on one over another enhances their ability to become experts in their methodology. And some causes are served better by one grant type over another. Using the kind of grant most appropriate to the request makes philanthropy more interesting.

---

32 "Program-Related Investing: Skills and Strategies for New PRI Funders," *GrantCraft*, http://www.grantcraft.org/?pageid=1297

9 | FUN AND EASY GIVING STRATEGIES

We've talked about the what, the how to choose, and the choice itself. We've walked through an overview of how to do grantmaking in a private foundation. Now for more detail on that "how" question. What grantmaking strategies (not types of grants) will be most appropriate for your goals? In other words, what works?

Responsive vs. Targeted Grantmaking

Many small or start-up foundations decide not to accept uninvited proposals. This choice is made because of uncertainty or even fear. By inviting only a few nonprofits to apply, these foundations believe they are avoiding wading through an unmanageable number of applications. It is debatable whether they would be inundated if they've instituted some of the issue and geographic focusing recommending in earlier chapters, but the concern is real and it has some basis in fact.

Practicing targeted philanthropy can be done in several ways. You can invite chosen nonprofits to send you an application. Or you may rely on your past relationship with that nonprofit and have a casual phone conversation. Sometimes folks will reduce the number of applicants by sending out requests for proposals (RFPs) that ask a few pre-selected nonprofits to decide if they are interested in providing a specific set of services or serve a specific clientele you are interested in supporting. If you don't accept unsolicited proposals, you risk not learning about effective nonprofits that you'd be very happy to support if you knew about them

Responsive grantmaking does have its pluses. If you decide to accept proposals from an open or fairly large cadre of applicants, you will learn more about the field(s) you fund. You can get jazzed about new approaches you've not heard about and find out about dozens or more nonprofits that you didn't know existed. It also gives the nonprofit sector in your focus area hope that there is a possibility that you may fund them. Not using an open and competitive application process may cause some people to think of private foundations as "playthings of the rich."[33] With an open process, however, you'll need to spend more time reviewing proposals.

Find Out What Works

Maybe you're interested in donating to help address a major problem in your community, but you aren't sure what the biggest need may be. There are many ways to find out. If you're a natural researcher, dig into the information on the Internet. Meet with the editor of your local newspaper. Talk with the community foundation staff. If there is an association of nonprofits, meet with their executive director. Call up the city, county, or even state departments of social services, health, education, and community development. Meet with the executive directors of the nonprofits you already support. Sit down with your local elementary, middle or high school principal. Contact your regional association of grantmakers.

Tell your story to anyone who might have worthwhile information to share. You might say, "I'm starting to donate funds to support improvement in my community in a more organized fashion. I'd like to learn what the real problems are and the various attempts to solve them. Can you suggest someone I can talk to who can give me an overview so I know where to invest my money?" You'll be surprised how willing people are to share what they've learned — especially if you admit to knowing very little to begin with!

---

[33] Congress did so in 1969, leading to most of the restrictions now placed on private foundations as a way to ensure distribution that helps society. The accusation has been repeated in newspaper articles in more recent times, leading to more discussions about increasing the payout requirement and requring foundations to spend out.

The terms "best" or "evidence-based practices" are often bandied about. Wouldn't it be wonderful if everything we do to change the world were proven to be effective? Some fields — typically medical, health, various social services, and education — actually can point to research that may help you identify which nonprofits are using such practices. A university or college may be a good source for such research; asking the nonprofit applicants what they base their strategies on is another. Such practices can help you craft the criteria you may use to make decisions in certain issue areas. Do be aware, however, that what works in one community may not, for a myriad of reasons, work in another. Listening to those who are on the ground doing the actual work is often one of the best ways to learn what works — and doesn't.

Some organizations actually cater to grantmakers, helping them identify best practices. An example: Grantmakers for Effective Organizations (http://www.geo.org) is a membership association that has commissioned research into the types of support grantmakers can offer nonprofits to increase recipients' effectiveness. Providing funding for capacity building (leadership and management skills, fundraising and technology, and information system development), for general operating costs (staff salaries, overhead, etc.) and multi-year support all build a nonprofit's ability to adapt to change and focus on providing services. Other resources: Practice Matters: The Improving Philanthropy Project (http://foundationcenter.org/gainknowledge/practicematters) offers advice aimed at foundations to consider ways to improve their practice of philanthropy at a more overarching level. Family foundations should take a look at the National Center for Family Philanthropy (http://www.ncfp.org). And Give Smart, a project of the Bridgespan Group (a nonprofit consulting firm), has an online Philanthropy Toolkit (http://www.givesmart.org/tools.aspx) with useful questions and other information.

These latter organizations attempt to identify best practices in philanthropy (types of support, application and review processes, etc.), not necessarily what are best practices in K-12 education or breaking the cycle of homelessness. There are "affinity groups" that may help you generally with your topics of interest, such as Grantmakers for Education (http://www.edfunders.org) or Grantmakers in the Arts (http://www.gia.org). Talking to their staff may lead you to useful research and to recommendations of people to speak with — generally funders known for their innovative or significant funding in the affinity group's area.

One of the easiest ways to gather best practices is to invite several people to participate in a discussion with you or your foundation's board of trustees. Commission (yes, pay them — it can count toward your payout requirement) a short "white paper" from nonprofit executive directors about the problem they're addressing and what might truly solve it. Ask them what they'd do with, say another $10,000 or $50,000 or half a million dollars. Ask them who they respect in the field and how they chose their strategies. And attend workshops, webinars and conferences.

Does this sound like too much work? This is the fun part! Learning is always interesting, and here you are in a position to soak up information from the experts. Over time you'll hear the same names arise or organizations noted approvingly. This will allow you to move toward those people and organizations that have gained the respect of experts and peers alike.

If you haven't time or interest to do this part of the work, any number of philanthropy consultants like me (or perhaps your son, daughter, or grandchild) would leap at the opportunity to investigate for you and neatly summarize opportunities for you to consider.

Sorry, Online Charity Evaluators Are Not (Yet) a Short Cut

There are several nonprofit online charity evaluators. Some are free, others charge for their services. They include:

- Charity Navigator
- Charity Watch
- GiveWell
- Giving What We Can
- Great Nonprofits
- Philanthropedia
- Root Cause
- BBB Wise Giving Alliance

At this point, most of the free online charity evaluators anoint a nonprofit with top ratings for its financial stinginess: Can they accomplish their mission on as little money as possible? Especially, can they manage to spend virtually nothing on overhead (rent, utilities, staffing, fundraising costs, technology, etc.) and still provide services that are successful in addressing some of the most intractable problems faced by society? Okay, so maybe you can tell where I come down on this.

They focus mostly on the financial side of the equation, because it's much easier to look at a nonprofit's tax return and develop a set of stats on their financials. Program and effectiveness information is less available on the IRS Form 990, and it's very difficult for an outsider without access to detailed data to review programmatic impact. Certainly these charity evaluators all talk about how important it is to look at the program side (and recently GuideStar, Charity Navigator and the BBB Wise Giving Alliance released a joint letter called "It's Time to Move Beyond Overhead"), but none have yet found a way to include much program information in their ratings. Charity Navigator plans on launching something in 2016 that holds promise, but these ratings should not take the place of good, old fashioned due diligence. Deciding whether to use Philanthropedia (which relies on recommendations from experts) or Root Cause (which analyzes social impact and compares to benchmarks) is a financial decision on your part because they charge for their reports.

A Lesson About "Overhead"

Overhead costs are worth a look. But each industry has a different level of necessary overhead, and not all nonprofits are in the same industry. A museum has very different overhead expenses from an afterschool arts program, for example. Most online charity evaluators (and for that matter, United Way chapters and private funders) think that the overhead figure should be limited to 15% or 20% — and certainly no more than 35% — of every nonprofit's budget. Yes, nonprofit organizations don't exist to create a profit distributed to shareholders, but that doesn't mean they shouldn't have the tools necessary to do their business. And that includes staff members who are talented and compensated fairly, including benefits. In fact, since some nonprofits rely so heavily on staff members who tend to have the talent to be either a jack of all trades or exceptional in their performance, I'd argue that working to attract and retain excellent staff in nonprofits is even more important than it is in for-profit endeavors.

HOW A CAPACITY BUILDING GRANT
LED TO USEFUL LEARNING

The Cedarmere Foundation is a family foundation focusing on families, children, social services and education through capacity building grants designed to enable small nonprofits to better fulfill their missions. Among their grants, they have provided small amounts to allow a number of executive directors to attend trainings, work with a coach or earn certificates in nonprofit leadership, fundraising, etc.

Kathy Edwards, Cedarmere's donor and president, thought it would be nice to invite those executive directors together to talk over what they've been learning and more about their struggles. This executive director peer exchange has now become formalized into an every other month brown bag lunch where the executive director hosting the meeting asks the group for feedback and discussion on a topic or two of particular relevance to her/ his organization. Others are free to submit their own topics for discussion as time allows at each meeting. These peer exchanges have proved so popular, that previous grantees of the Cedarmere Foundation asked to continue attending.

Kathy and her husband, George, himself a retired nonprofit executive, also attend and recalled when they started to dive deeply into problems. "Somebody brought up a topic that clearly one could have read as reflecting negatively on their organization. Another said, 'Gosh, maybe we shouldn't talk about our failures in front of our funders.' A third person immediately piped up, 'There's nothing wrong with that; Cedarmere's our partner and they want us to succeed!' That really validated our grantees' trust in us."

Kathy and George believe the foundation's peer exchange meetings have been valuable to both the foundation and to its grantees. "It makes us feel like we've been able to leverage our small grant dollars even more significantly because of what the executive directors of our grantee organizations gain from each other and we've learned more about our grantees in the peer exchanges than from any other interaction we have with them."

Did you know that 75% of nonprofit executive directors plan to leave their jobs within five years — and 17% of those have either already given notice (7%) or are seriously considering it (10%)?[34] Aren't the goals of nonprofits at least as important as manufacturing a widget or providing a for-profit service? I think it's very important for donors to avoid using a "magic" overhead percentage (especially since there isn't one that fits every nonprofit, just as there isn't one that fits every industry) and think

---

[34] From Cornelius, Marla, Rick Moyers, and Jeanne Bell, *Daring to Lead 2011: A National Study of Executive Director Leadership* (San Francisco, CA: CompassPoint Nonprofit Services and the Meyer Foundation, 2011). Download or review at www.daringtolead.org.

they're making a smart investment if they automatically select the one that appears to spend less on overhead.

Why? To fundraise successfully, nonprofits are practiced at crafting the percentages to make them look as good as possible. What you see on the organization's 990 tax return or in Charity Navigator, *et al.*, may be negotiable depending on who is interpreting what's a program vs. fundraising vs. administrative expense. Also, all things being equal, you could contrast one nonprofit with another, and the one with a lower overhead may be reaching fewer clients or customers due to antiquated technology, spending days moving and re-moving inventory after five floods in a year (honest, a real story), or on the verge of collapse because of inadequate staff. They may look good on paper. Just don't use that overhead percentage as the gold standard for rating a nonprofit's effectiveness or worthiness of support. Besides, shouldn't everyone be compensated according to his or her expertise and skill? Is it really appropriate that three-quarters of nonprofit CEOs are paid between $50,000 and $75,000, even after a successful tenure of decades?

Fix the System Rather Than Band-Aid® the Result

In examining what works, one of the important lessons to learn while practicing philanthropy is that change is hard. If it were easy, would we have all the problems in society that we struggle with? Systems created to address issues (school systems, human services, health care) are usually large, cumbersome, and fragile. Let's fix the system!

Well, how?

Certainly there are efficiencies that can be gained and technologies that can help. But to truly change a system usually means that government must be involved. And that means advocacy.

"But," I hear you ask, "didn't my attorney say I couldn't do anything that might be thought of as lobbying as a private foundation?" Likely, he or she did. But no rule says you can't support nonprofits that *do* lobby. Not that you'd provide a grant specifically *for* lobbying. You can't do *indirectly* what you aren't allowed to do directly. You're not lobbying if you provide a general operating grant to a 501(c)(3) public charity that performs the permissible amount of lobbying (see Chapter 14) to improve laws and regulations that affect their ability to serve their clientele. You can't change a system without advocating for change.

Of course you can always contact your elected officials and regulators as an individual or representing your business. Just make it clear you are *not* representing your private foundation. But another important way to let folks know what you do *is to tell them.* Print an annual report. Set up a meeting with your state legislator or Member of Congress to share your passions and concerns. As long as you are not endorsing or criticizing specific legislation before the body in question, you are *educating.* And it is important that all levels of government understand the role of philanthropy if for no other reason than to prevent them from deciding that you and your philanthropic peers can take the place of government in funding good causes. (The total amount of philanthropic giving in a year totaled $316.23 billion in 2012, most of which came from individuals through direct donations, bequests, and family foundations. Sounds like a lot. But it represents only 2% of GDP.[35] There's no practical way private philanthropy can replace government.) Note an interesting exception: there is no limit on seeking to influence government *agencies* regarding legislation.

What's "New" in Philanthropy?

Philanthropy, like any other field or industry, goes through changes, trends, and cycles. Charity was originally seen pretty much as a way to help people who were hungry, who needed shelter, or who begged on the street for a handout of a coin or two. In the United States, John D. Rockefeller (1839-1937) and Andrew Carnegie (1835-1919) both played large roles in adding to the ways people thought about philanthropy. Rockefeller turned to a systematic approach of funding education and science to undergird major changes in society, such as the Green Revolution (which saved millions of lives) and establishing the University of Chicago from the ground up. Carnegie believed in partnering with communities by building and equipping libraries only when the communities first agreed to purchase the land and pay for the library's staffing and upkeep into the future. Both played large roles in altering how people thought about philanthropy, moving beyond just giving alms to the poor.

---

[35] From *Giving USA Report 2013: The Annual Report on Philanthropy,*
http://www.givingusareports.org/

More recently, we've tried to find root causes to problems as a way to address them before they blossom. Can we prevent the problems from occurring in the first place? People with a desire to approach philanthropy from this perspective tend to fund nonprofits using early intervention concepts. Examples include efforts to strengthen early-childhood education; upstream programs such as mental health courts to treat people rather than jail them; or a program where nurses mentor young, low-income pregnant women through the child's second birthday. The development of good public policy and the field of prevention science are also designed to stop problems before they start.

The current trend and controversy in philanthropy is over the idea that nonprofits should be managed more like for-profits, to result, supposedly, in a more sustainable, efficient and successful service model. Some donors like to think of their philanthropy as "venture philanthropy" or "philanthrocapitalism," which uses concepts from venture investment to help shape charitable investment choices. Some of these concepts — many of which are also used by foundations not calling themselves venture philanthropists — are:

- High engagement (of the donor in the activities of nonprofit grantees)
- Tailored financing (loans, grants, hybrids of the two)
- Multi-year support (average 5-7 years)
- Organizational capacity building (to enhance the long-term viability of the organization)
- Performance measurement (with an emphasis on business planning, measurable outcomes, and achievement of milestones)[36]
- Encouragement of the use of market forces to strengthen organizational sustainability

There are some problems with this current trend. As I'll note in Chapter 14, nonprofits are different from for-profits. Judy Vredenburgh, a former for-profit business leader and nonprofit CEO, said it succinctly:

Every time we in nonprofits satisfy customers, we drain resources, and every time for-profits satisfy a customer, they get resources back. That sounds very simple, but it has huge

---

[36] From "Venture Philanthropy, Defined," Social Innovation Europe, https://webgate.ec.europa.eu/socialinnovationeurope/magazine/finance/articles-reports/venture-philanthropy-defined

implications, and I don't think the for-profit people really get that.[37]

Bruce Sievers, former executive director of the Walter and Elise Haas Foundation, voiced another aspect of this issue:

An analogy would be to think of the primary point of participating in sports as winning a gold medal at the Olympics, rather than the intrinsic value of the participation itself. In civil society, as in sports, the means matter as much as the ends, because in many ways the values embodied in the means are the ends.

So my primary point is that relationships with the market and the "business model" pose dangers for civil society. We're not just producers of solutions to social problems. And I would say this to funders even more than to nonprofits: don't fixate on "measurable outcomes" or "scale" or "effectiveness" to the exclusion of supporting the mixture of ideals, motivations, compassion, and human interactions that constitute the essential quality of civil society organizations.[38]

There are studies about returns on social investment and cost per individual helped to attempt to measure change and efficiency in the nonprofit sector. Micro-enterprise and crowd-sourced funding (see Kiva Zip at https://zip.kiva.org/loans) — a new donor-directed microloan program for U.S. entrepreneurs) are new ways to institute old ideas. There are even efforts (mostly at the state levels) to develop hybrid corporate structures that more easily allow for social benefit businesses to operate (e.g., the L3C, or low-profit limited liability corporation, the benefit corporation, and the flexible or social purpose corporation). And some venture philanthropists are taking their commitment to venture capital investing to new heights. Read a fascinating May 17, 2013 article by Brad Reagan in the *Wall Street Journal* called "The New Science of Giving" about a Houston couple planning on giving away $4 billion to organizations that scientifically prove they are successful.

---

[37] Les Silverman and Lynn Taliento, "What Business Execs Don't Know — But Should — About Nonprofits," *Stanford Social Innovation Review*, Summer 2006.

[38] "A Tale of Three Cities" by Bruce Sievers, *Linkages*, Spring 2006, Rockefeller Philanthropy Advisors. From a speech given March 21, 2006 at the annual meeting of the California Association of Nonprofits.

I think it's fair to acknowledge that venture philanthropy has provided a number of effective concepts to the field of philanthropy, especially multi-year engagement and capacity building. There are, however, inherent disparities between nonprofit and for-profit work, mostly having to do with the amount of resources available, hierarchies and decision-making systems that are more or less complex, the number of stakeholders to keep happy, and the greater or lesser ability to measure performance. All philanthropists will do well to understand the purpose of nonprofits and their history and culture, as well as to develop a clear concept of how they wish to aid nonprofits in their endeavors.

Evaluate Your Results

It bears repeating: The only way to know if you've accomplished what you intended is to first identify what you intend to accomplish. Then ascertain how to gather the information that can reveal what has actually occurred.

A whole industry has sprung up around the field of evaluation in the nonprofit sector. Government grants have required quantitative evaluation for many years. Consultants and universities teach nonprofits and funders alike about how to develop and then present (visually through a "logic model")[39] their theories of change.[40]

Don't worry — this can be simpler than it sounds, and there are online plug and play tools to help you. But if you do not plan to invest in the development of your own theory of change, you may find that pre-planning your grantmaking strategies together with an extremely simple set of questions asked of your grant recipients can be sufficient. Spend the time necessary before making a grant deciding which grantmaking methods (funding general operating or advocacy, providing multi-year support) you feel are most useful. You can then be assured that your dollars are making some impact.

---

[39] A logic model is a visual planning tool to clarify and graphically display what your project intends to do and what it hopes to accomplish and impact.

[40] The Center for the Theory of Change (http://www.theoryofchange.org) states: "a Theory of Change defines all building blocks required to bring about a given long-term goal. This set of connected building blocks – interchangeably referred to as outcomes, results, accomplishments, or preconditions – is depicted on a map known as a pathway of change/change framework, which is a graphic representation of the change process."

I encourage people to call nonprofit executive directors with these questions. The call can lead to interesting discussions. Another technique is to ask their grantees to respond in writing at the end of the grant period (usually a year). The questions are simply:

1. What did you do?
2. What did you learn?
3. What would you do differently next time?

Note that these questions don't necessarily require a lot of data or numbers. They tend to bring forth a summary and some anecdotal stories. But that can be enough for you as a funder to determine if your grant was useful either in terms of serving the nonprofits' clients or learning something new.

The key to making this information useful is that you record it, read it, think about it, and determine if your decisions will change in the future as a result of that information.

Asking your grantees to track certain measurements and write up long evaluation reports can be the right thing to do if you've supported their work with a large, multi-year grant and if they have the capacity to undertake such tracking (or if you've funded them to do so — especially at their request). But most grants, especially small grants, can't make systemic change occur. Nor can a foundation necessarily identify what *they* accomplished because of a $1,000, $5,000, or $10,000 grant.

For more on evaluation, see Chapter 12.

Experiment!

Some people believe that they waste precious and limited resources if they don't, prior to investing, research the best methods and recipients. The co-donor or trustee of a large family foundation said in a meeting I attended that she believed the nonprofit sector is too important to "experiment on" and that the pre-work and thought that went into the operations of her and her husband's foundation's were vital to its success and the values they hold. I admire her dedication. And I have seen donors who, I admit, seem to toy with grant applicants and recipients — and their own values — by constantly changing their focus areas or leading some applicants along by encouraging their applications when they know ahead of time the chance of funding that applicant is miniscule. But I think that some experimentation can be a good way to enter the philanthropic arena. It's a fast track to learn in a hands-on manner. And particularly if you have little patience for "book learning," experimenting can lead you to grantmaking methods that work well for you.

10 | APPLICATIONS AND THE ART OF CHOOSING A GRANT RECIPIENT

Accepting All Proposals vs. Inviting Proposals Only

This decision is often made solely on the basis of staffing. Do you or your staff, if any, have enough time to review what might come to your email in-box or your snail-mail mailbox? I think this question deserves more consideration than that.

Why does any foundation accept proposals? It's the most open way to learn about nonprofits that are doing good work in the focus areas of your shared interest. It is unlikely if you grant in a geographic area larger than a small town or rural county that you are aware of all the nonprofits in your region. You certainly don't know all the nonprofits in the nation! New nonprofits pop up all the time. And isn't it part of your responsibility as a philanthropist to learn about the vehicles you can support in achieving good works?

That doesn't mean you must openly entertain all proposals that come your way, especially if you aren't staffed for it and your grantmaking budget is relatively small. As previously discussed, you can constrain what comes through your door in a number of ways:

1. Limit your geographic reach. By doing so, the number of nonprofits eligible for potential funding will be constrained to those 501(c)(3) organizations and other entities you can legally give to that are located in that region. (Of course you must advertise publicly just what those geographic restrictions are.)

2. Limit the issues you fund. Ditto.

3. Choose a strategy within an issue and fund only within that strategy. (Fund only nonprofits working with low-income children by providing mentors or other adults in their lives — an intensive but proven strategy.)

4. Invite one-page only letters of inquiry that summarize the potential request and invite full applications only from those that hit the mark for you. (A lot less reading.)

5. Allow only nonprofits with budgets of a certain range to apply: really small ones of less than $500,000, less than $1 million, from $1 and 5 million, etc.

6. Exclude a variety of types of grants or organizations, depending on their interests. Common exclusions include religious institutions, start-ups, capital gifts, and organizations that operate solely for their own members' benefit.

Or you can decide, after thinking about it, that you can't or don't wish to accept unsolicited applications. This means you should spend time in the community searching out good organizations that fit your guidelines. Talk to your friends. Attend arts and cultural events. Invite family to nominate nonprofits they think you should investigate. Do web searches and read the newspaper. Revisit your past donations. Learn from experts and nonprofit leaders. And then invite applications only from those that you think have a good chance of matching your interests and criteria. You can still use a two-step process (letter of inquiry first, then invite a full proposal, which can cut down on the number of proposals you must review).

Questions You Should — and Shouldn't — Ask

If you plan on asking questions of potential grant recipients prior to awarding them a grant, you need to decide how to do this. An application form is a typical method, as is a list of questions you want answered, which can be easier for the nonprofit if the form can be filled out and submitted online. (Remember, no one has a typewriter anymore.) In either case, you ask questions to gain information that will help you make an informed decision.

There are three overarching "do's and don'ts" to follow regarding what questions to ask:

1. Don't ask for more information than you'll use to help you make a decision. Even if you think you *should* ask for a detailed financial statement, don't ask for it if you don't really intend to analyze it.
2. Do scale the number of questions you ask to the size of grant you plan on making. If you make grants in the $10,000 or less range, you shouldn't require applicants to spend as much time and effort filling out an application or answering questions as they would if they were asking for $50,000 or $100,000. Or more.
3. Consider using a regional common application form. You can find links to those that exist at the Foundation Center. Several regional associations of grantmakers have crafted common forms that multiple grantmakers use, (possibly) making it easier for applicants. But you may not need answers to all the questions on the common form. You can add a cover note identifying which questions to skip, or if you must, add questions.

AN EASY BUT STILL-USEFUL APPLICATION PROCESS

Years ago I came to know a family foundation trustee who dumbfounded me by stating, "We accept any kind of application the nonprofit wants to send; including ones sent to other foundations." This was an inspired idea. The foundation was relatively new and not wedded at the time to set of criteria. But the trustee was loath to put pressure on applicants by requiring more information than was needed. So why not allow applicants to send an already written application and avoid wasting time inserting the foundation's name in each place it was mentioned? The Tauck Family Foundation now has a more developed philanthropy and an application process that includes requests for proposals. But what a great idea — and one that worked well at the time!

OK, What Do I Need to Know?

You will want to collect three types of information: basic contact information; what, exactly, are they asking you to support; and information that you'll use over time to gauge progress. A typical list of desired information may include some of the following:

For obvious reasons:
1. Name of organization
2. Contact name and title
3. Address
4. Phone/email
5. Website URL
6. Amount requested

To simplify your record keeping:
7. Title of grant request
8. Summary of grant request

For decision-making purposes:
9. Organization's mission statement or purpose
10. Statement of needs
11. Who, where, and number served
12. Organization's accomplishments and qualifications
13. Goals, objectives, timeline, anticipated impact
14. Evaluation plan: How will success be monitored and measured
15. Financial statements (balance sheet, income/expense statement, operating budget, audited financial statements)
16. Other current and potential funders
17. Proof of 501(c)(3) and public charity status
18. List of board members and their affiliations

Some funders ask applicants to attach various documents, including informational brochures, annual reports, detailed project budgets (especially if seeking funding for large capital purposes or separate projects), and even copies of their IRS 990s.[41]

But Don't Ask All These Questions All the Time!

Especially for smaller grants, ask only the questions for which you want answers. Don't use a lengthy list of questions to determine if the nonprofit is really serious about their application! Some donors rely on a nonprofit's website to answer many of these questions (especially

---

[41] I don't recommend requiring copies of the nonprofit's IRS 990 tax return. They're long and expensive to copy and mail. If you want to take a look, it's easy to do so online via GuideStar.org or the Foundation Center at FoundationCenter.org.

numbers 9, 10, 11, 13, 15, 16 and 18). After time, you may not feel a need to ask a long-time grant recipient to provide you the basics but will request only information about organizational changes, the new project, or lessons learned.[42]

Those Pesky Financials

Ah, yes. Financials. If you come from the business world, it is possible that financial statements are a font of information for you. But you still may be a bit confused since nonprofit accounting is different from for-profit accounting. The key difference is that nonprofits use fund accounting, which focuses on accountability rather than profitability, tracking sources of funding and their use. If math isn't your strong suit, financial statements may obscure rather than illuminate. Let's talk briefly about the various kinds of statements.

Statement of financial position (similar to a balance sheet): This shows a snapshot of the financial health of a nonprofit at one point in time. For example, on this date, the nonprofit has this much money in the bank, is owed this much, has liabilities (current, long-term) of this much, restricts this much for specific projects, and has this much total in net assets (current, fixed, long-term). Seeing balance sheets over a two to three year period can give you a sense of the organization's financial direction. Remember that not all organizations, private foundations included, use a calendar year. This can make it even more difficult to ensure the nonprofit is receiving dollars when it actually needs it, vs. when its annual meeting happens to occur.

The bit that can be confusing for those who are used to seeing a for-profit's balance sheet are the restrictions put on funds. When you as a donor provide a capital grant to build a building, or a grant for a specific or new program, the nonprofit must place those funds on its statements as "temporarily restricted." So too are gifts given with a time restriction. When they are used for the purpose for which they were donated, those funds are then "unrestricted." When a gift to an endowment is made, those funds are typically "permanently restricted" so they can be used for the purpose of providing ongoing revenue, as was intended. The nonprofit's board can also temporarily restrict monies for a certain use,

---

[42] See Project Streamline (http://www.projectstreamline.org) for more information about how to streamline your application and reporting process.

but they are listed as part of the "unrestricted" pot because the board can change its mind at any time. The nonprofit, however, cannot change the donor's intent.

Statement of financial activities (similar to an income/expense statement):[43] This shows how much income — and from what sources, such as "earned" or "contributed" — has come in in the past year compared to current income in the year-to-date. It also shows where the money has been spent and on what function or activity within the same time frame. Sometimes a budget column (see operating budget below) is added so that one can see how close-to-budget the organization managed its revenue and expenses over a period of time. A very complete view may include columns with the prior year actual, current year to date, current year budget, percent of budget to date, year-end forecast, budget to year-end variance, and notes. Many nonprofits won't include all of these in their statements.

Operating budget: Each year every organization budgets what it believes its income and expenses will be. This, again, is a snapshot in time of what the nonprofit's best guess was when that budget was adopted before the beginning of the current fiscal year. Variances are expected; so don't judge an organization solely on whether it sticks to its budget figures. It's the year-end trend over several years that tells more.

Detailed budgets: If the nonprofit operates several programs or projects, each usually has its own budget, likely in more detail than the organization's budget as a whole. If you are funding a particular program or project, you'll probably want to see that budget just to make sure it seems sensible. Capital projects and social enterprises can have multiple budgets, especially when construction is involved.

Audited financial statements: A lot of foundations ask for audited financial statements. This is when a CPA reviews the balance sheet, income/expense statements, operating budgets, bank accounts, invoices, board meeting minutes, and financial practices. It is certainly good practice for any organization to have an independent auditor review its financial statements and protocols on an annual basis to ensure its systems are strong. But did you know that an audit might cost as much as $10,000? As a result, smaller nonprofits may not conduct an audit each year but instead do so every two or three years. They may participate in a less-thorough procedure called a "review" that may suffice for your purposes. And many small nonprofits rely on an independent bookkeeper to

---

[43] For-profits call their equivalent statement, "Profit and Loss."

provide "outside" financial controls. You may wish to ask for the latest audited financial statement, but it may not be necessary to *require* one. If you have no interest in the full audit, you could ask for a copy of the management letter that is attached to an audit listing any recommended changes to the nonprofit's financial system and set of controls and ask what they've done to implement the recommendations for improvement. If there are no recommendations, there will be no management letter. (That's actually a good thing.)

I recommend you think about how you look at financial statements, whether you understand what they tell you, and how they weigh into your decision-making process. Asking your own bookkeeper or CPA to give you a tutorial, or even to review a financial statement from an applicant, can't hurt. You can even ask your own CPA/bookkeeping firm if it would, as a favor, provide an audit on a *pro bono* basis to a nonprofit you support! (But make sure they have some nonprofit accounting experience, first.)

Some useful examples and "how to" information for both you and the nonprofits you fund can be found at Nonprofit Accounting Basic$ (http://www.nonprofitaccountingbasics.org/).

Learning From Financial Statements:
Good Information or Gobbledygook?

I recommend using the questions and strategies from Financial SCAN (http://www.guidestar.org/rxg/products/nonprofit-data-solutions/financial-scan.aspx), developed by the Nonprofit Finance Fund and GuideStar. They provide spiffy graphs, charts, and ratios that allow you to compare the financials of one nonprofit against as many as five other similar ones. Financial SCAN allows you to see measurements (taken from IRS Form 990 tax returns, so the information is as old as the last Form 990 filed) that include personnel costs, expense categories and estimated full costs, revenue composition, earned income and contributed revenue, a profitability graph showing unrestricted surplus or deficit, balance sheet composition graphs, and liquidity graphs (that show the number of months of expenses covered by the money they have available — liquidity). Note that you can actually subscribe to Financial SCAN and have them do all the work, which is quite a nice timesaver. But it's an investment. Here are the questions that Financial SCAN[44] answers to enable you to determine the financial health of a nonprofit. You can ask them yourself.

- What have been sources of contributed revenue?
- Has the organization covered its costs?
- Has the asset distribution changed over time?
- Does the organization own land, buildings, or equipment?
- How have assets been financed?
- How has the distribution of liabilities changed over time?
- What has been the composition of net assets?
- Has the organization had adequate access to cash?

Remember that I mentioned in Chapter 9 that overhead is a good thing? Here is Social Velocity's blog comment by Nell Edgington (http://www.socialvelocity.net) that resonates with me. It does a good job explaining why looking for that administrative/program ratio cost isn't useful. It lists "X% of your donation goes to the program" as one of five lies to stop telling donors:

> The distinction between "program expenses" and "overhead" is, at best, meaningless and, at worst, destructive. You cannot have a program without staff, technology, space, systems, evaluation, and research and development. It is magical thinking to say that you can separate money spent on programs from money spent on the support of programs. Donors need to understand, and you need to explain to them, that "overhead" is not a dirty word. A nonprofit exists to deliver programs. And *everything* the organization does help to make those programs better, stronger, bigger, more effective.[45]

Also see Nonprofit Financial Ratios (https://nonprofitsassistancefund.org/sites/default/files/publications/nonprofit_financial_ratios_2013.pdf) where nearly 15 ratios are listed, only one of which is the typically used (but less useful) ratio of functional cost

---

[44] From http://www.guidestar.org/ViewCmsFile.aspx?ContentID=4232.

[45] From *Financing, Not Fundraising: 5 Lies to Stop Telling Donors,* http://www.socialvelocity.net/2011/10/financing-not-fundraising-5-lies-to-stop-telling-donors

allocation (the ratio of administrative cost to a particular functional cost). And the Nonprofit Finance Fund (http://www.nonprofitfinancefund.org/innovative-practice-groups) offers grantmakers workshops on "how to assess grantees' key financial indicators and understand their critical business needs."

Proof of 501(c)(3) and Public Charity Status

Many foundations ask for a copy of the organization's 501(c)(3) IRS determination letter. You must *read* the letter to see if it addresses whether the organization is a public charity or other 501(c) category. For the most up to date information (whether their letter has been revoked, for instance), you can pay to enroll in GuideStar's Charity Check (http://www.guidestar.org/rxg/products/verification-solutions/guidestar-charity-check.aspx) verification service or look on the IRS website for the current information (updated monthly) at EO (Exempt Organizations) Select Check (http://www.irs.gov/Charities-&-Non-Profits/Search-for-Charities).

Did They Do What They Said They Would With the Donation?

Ask them. Some foundations require a report on the program, project, or organization's progress that was aided by their funding. This is usually called a "report back" and can be required at the end of the grant period or even periodically if it is a large or lengthy grant. Some foundations will even refuse to provide another grant to an organization if they don't provide the report back.

This report can be a discussion held in-person or on the phone, or in written form. Remember that you can keep it very simple. Here's a repeat of the questions to ask your grantee to address:

- What did you do?
- What did you learn?
- What will you do differently next time?

Other Applications: RFPs, RFQs, LOIs

An RFP is a request for a proposal; RFQ is a request for qualifications; and LOI stands for letter of interest or letter of inquiry. The only reason you need to know is that these documents represent a step in the grantmaking process that you may (or may not) wish to include in your application practice.

Let's start with the one used most often: LOI. LOIs briefly summarize an applicant's proposal and are used to allow grantmakers to winnow down the number of full applications they must review and to increase the odds that what they do receive meets their criteria. LOIs also give the funder an idea of which nonprofits have interest in responding with a proposal. Usually an LOI is required to be short (1-2 pages long), pointed (what exactly is your project/request and for how much), and investigatory ("might you be interested in funding this?"). The idea is that applicants won't spend hours and hours preparing full proposals and grantmakers won't spend hours and hours reading full proposals unless the applicant first makes it through the much less time-intensive LOI stage.

Foundations use requests for proposals (or qualifications) when they have a strong interest in a particular issue, project, or type of work. For instance, here's an example of a (very) simple RFP taken right off the Foundation Center's Request for Proposals web page in June 2013 (http://foundationcenter.org/pnd/rfp):

Pedigree Foundation Invites Applications for 2013 Innovation and Operation Grant

The Pedigree Foundation is accepting applications for its 2013 Innovation and Operation Grants program from nonprofit animal shelters and dog rescue groups.

Innovation grants ranging from $10,000 to $25,000 will be awarded to organizations that have successfully deployed creative animal shelter or dog rescue programs. Grants of up to $1,000 will be awarded to provide financial aid to shelters and rescue groups to help fund basic operating needs.

To be eligible, applicant organizations must be a tax-exempt nonprofit shelter or rescue group, organizationally stable, and able to demonstrate an ability to collaborate/partner within the community to promote, educate, and/or increase awareness of issues that contribute to dog homelessness.

See the Pedigree Foundation Web site for eligibility and application guidelines.

RFPs are sometimes quite complicated. Scientific and health research awards often use RFPs. But if you are looking for the best applications from interested eligible organizations in, for example, teaching critical thinking skills through arts in K-12 education, an RFP can be an extremely useful tool.

11 | ONCE UPON A TIME...
WHY TELLING YOUR STORY IS IMPORTANT

Many family foundations pursue their work under a cloak of
darkness. Not as in evil darkness but as in "let's not
advertise what we do because we'll be inundated by
requests" kind of darkness. Believe me, I understand that fear. I also
know that some people believe giving anonymously or without fanfare is a
religious or ethical choice they make.

But I think foundations have a responsibility to share what they've
learned.

Think of it this way: Sharing what you learn is the rent you pay for the
ability to direct your donations even after you've received your tax break.
You are now stewards of the money that you (or an ancestor) dedicated to
the public good. In many ways it is no longer yours. You can't take it
back. You can't benefit personally from it. But except for the IRS,
Congress, and some state officials, no one else tells you what you can do
with the money in your foundation.

As a result, your job is to give thoughtfully and share those thoughts
with, at a minimum, your fellow trustees, family and peers. This way, they
learn with you. I think it is common courtesy also to share with those you
fund and to anyone else interested. An annual "lessons learned this year
about grantmaking in K-12 education" (for example), would be a breath

of fresh air. But at a minimum, you should review your grants annually, make an effort to learn about the issues you try to affect and the nonprofit sector you work through, and at least tell people what you've funded, how much and why.

Yes, what you've funded and for how much is public information, and anyone can get it off the Internet from your 990-PF tax return. It's the "why" part that requires a bit more effort to figure out the best way to communicate. It can be simple. Write up a short statement about who you are, the history of your foundation (why did you set one up?), what issues are of interest to you, how to apply (if applicable), a clear statement that you *don't* accept unsolicited proposals (if you don't), and lists of past grants. By including a bit of you, your passions and reasons for those passions, you are clarifying the "why" of what you do. You needn't have a set of criteria that you share (unless you have a set you wish to share), but you can inform everyone about your values.

Then, at the end of each year, send a letter and a list of your grants to all of your representatives in Congress, members of the state legislature, and others who might be interested in knowing what you've done in the communities you both serve. It can't hurt to remind the folks that set the regulations by which you must operate that you're doing good for the world — and, in particular, the portion of it that they also serve!

You Should Probably Have a Website

The easiest way to share this information widely is to have a website, even if you don't accept unsolicited proposals. All the information above can be posted on a free (except for miniscule hosting costs), simple website that you can produce yourself. See do-it-yourself website services like Weebly.com or Yola.com, among many others, or you can hire someone to do it for you. Another option is the free Foundation Center's "Foundation Folders" (http://www.foundationcenter.org/grantmakers/folders) that serve as websites. Post your statement and you're done.

Of course you can get more involved by blogging about your experiences (see Glasspockets: Bringing transparency to the world of philanthropy's list of 192 foundations that currently blog.)[46] Reflect annually on your grantees and what they've taught you, link back to each

---

[46] From http://maps.foundationcenter.org/glasspockets/transparency.php#Blog

grantee, invite comments, and even support a password-protected communication portal for your board members to comment back and forth. All of this is good. But my point is you don't have to do all or nothing. Even a one-page website can be a good choice.

If you are techno-phobic and can't bear the idea of owning a website, then I suggest you do two things. First, make sure you supply the Foundation Center and GuideStar with all of the information about your foundation: its purpose, its focus areas, values, strategies and procedures. Nonprofits often use Foundation Center and GuideStar to learn about potential funders, so make sure all necessary information is included in your listing. Second, make sure your IRS 990-PF tax return is complete. Think of the 990-PF as a public relations piece or as something that tells a story about your foundation and attach any information you'd like people to know about you.

Be Polite

"Do I have to answer phone calls from applicants?" I hear you ask with a bit of panic in your voice. No, you don't. It is certainly polite to do so if you have the staff capacity. By doing so you can become more in touch with what nonprofits need and you can help shape proposals to meet your decision criteria. But this is one of the things that many non-staffed foundations don't do. No office, no dedicated phone number. As I mentioned above, that means you have a responsibility to communicate to nonprofits about what you do and don't do in an easily accessible manner. If you want to go a step further, but don't have the time to answer calls, offer an e-mail address (with information about how often it is checked) and spend an hour or two a week (or a day a month?) responding. Here again, this can be a good place for hired help, a consultant, or a well-trained and trustworthy family member.

How to Say "No"

Quickly, compassionately, straightforwardly. If you deliver sad news via e-mail, say "Regrets from the X Foundation" in the subject line so they know right away. (This was a suggestion from a humorous but truth-speaking nonprofit executive director and blogger named Vu Le in an entry called "The art of giving bad news.")[47] It feels good to make phone

---

[47] See Vu Le's Blog, http://nonprofitwithballs.com

calls with *good* news, so don't deny yourself that joy.

You will be asked by some very disappointed executive or development directors why they weren't chosen, or for "suggestions to improve the request in the future." There are several ways to address this. First, put yourself in their shoes. Wouldn't you like to know why you didn't make the grade? Don't resent them for putting you in a position you'd rather not be.

No, I'm not forgetting about the subjectivity of grantmaking. It can be difficult to say "why" when "why" may not have a very good answer. And you may be stuck stating only that you received 72 proposals totaling $1.5M in requests and could fund only $152,000. But if you do have a reason why their application didn't make it to the top that you're willing to share, do so. Applicants will appreciate it. If you think you really aren't interested in ever supporting a particular organization, don't encourage them to apply next year. Tell them "it would be in your best interest to seek support elsewhere in the future."

Oh. That part about not feeling guilty? Good luck with that. Everyone realizes that you can't fund everything, but no one likes to be the sender or receiver of bad news. You may indeed feel guilt and not be able to make that part go away.

How to Say "Yes"
Without People Fawning All Over You

I seem to be saying, "you can't" a lot in this book, but you can't say yes without at least some people fawning over you. Nonprofits rely on you and your fellow philanthropists for their very survival. It's pretty difficult as a nonprofit leader not to be grateful for funding and to show it. And face it; if they weren't appreciative, would you want to give them grants in the future? What you want here is to be gracious ("We're very pleased to be able to offer you support of your excellent work") and to remember what nonprofits attempt to do in our communities is extremely difficult. They tackle the most intractable problems and try to fix them on a financial shoestring while constantly begging for support. It's *a lot* harder than giving away money. Be appreciative of their efforts, forgiving of their mistakes, and fund them in ways that help them become stable, strong, and eventually thriving public charities.

12 | MAKING A DIFFERENCE: CAN I REALLY KNOW?

Again, nope, sorry, you can't. "But making a difference is why I entered philanthropy!" I hear you cry. Why do I say that you can't know? Because you can't *prove* that your $10,000 is what made the *actual* difference in a nonprofit's success or failure to help someone climb out of poverty. Or to access childcare. Or to teach kids to play music. Or, or, or....

Years ago I was impressed by a lecture given by Emmy Werner, Ph.D., about a 40+ year longitudinal study of a 1955 Kauai cohort she'd been conducting on high-risk children to see how resilient they'd been and what protective factors may have contributed to that resiliency.[48] One of the major protective factors that was identified, one that could occur at any time in that person's life, was a positive relationship with an adult (as a child) and with others (as an adult). This was "proof." One could extrapolate that, for example, Big Brothers Big Sisters can help develop resiliency in high-risk children. But it took 42 years to "prove" it. And it wasn't necessarily only the Big Brothers Big Sisters program that helped; it could have been the youth pastor at the community church who paid attention. Or the neighbor who let the child inside her house after school when things at the child's home were too chaotic.

---

[48] Emmy Werner and Ruth S. Smith, *Overcoming the Odds: High Risk Children from Birth to Adulthood*, Cornell University Press, 1992; and *Journeys From Childhood to Midlife: Risk, Resilience and Recovery*, Cornell University Press, 2001.

If you are a funder who gives the Big Brothers Big Sisters a grant, you can certainly say that you think the organization is making a difference in kids' lives. But you can't actually say that *your* grant is what made that difference, since all children have many influences on their lives, for good or ill.

Now if you could afford to pay for a double blind study so that one group is given the intervention, another group is prevented from receiving the help, and all other factors are considered, analyzed, and accounted for, maybe you could actually prove something. But not many organizations can afford this kind of evaluation. And some might consider withholding potential aid ethically questionable.

Here's What You Can Know

You *can* know if the nonprofits you fund:

- Are financially stable and trending upward
- Have innovative, charismatic and experienced leadership
- Are staffed appropriately to the needs of the organization
- Have policies and systems in place that safeguard the organization as well as the recipients of aid
- Create and follow a thoughtful plan of action — and pay attention to whether it works
- Play well with others
- Understand the public policies needed to strengthen the environment in which they operate and that fighting for the right policies (and against bad ones) can be necessary
- Are aware of their mistakes, appreciate learning, and measure progress
- Are nimble enough to make mid-course corrections
- Can effectively communicate the purposes and methods they use to achieve their missions

You can also learn about "best practices" in the field you're funding. Most social services best practices now include mentoring, wrap-around services, individualized plans, and post-program assistance. All of these terms can be found and understood with a little research — both formal and informal, online or in person.

Evaluation Is Important, But...

Assessing progress is important. It's just not *always* do-able. Small nonprofits can't always afford to hire consultants to help them identify what to measure, ways to measure, gather data, analyze and learn from data, and then institute appropriate changes (which, after all, is the purpose of evaluation — it is *not* measurement for its own sake). Defining goals, measuring progress, and managing accordingly *sounds* so simple, doesn't it? But it can be fraught with danger for nonprofits. If they find what they've been doing isn't working, will they have the ability to change course? Will they lose their funders? Nonprofit leaders want to do what works. But demonstrating that their programs do work is not something that all nonprofits can afford or have the vision to do. And funders can't be too rigid — particularly with smaller and newer nonprofits — or they may destroy the ability of these organizations to grow and become more effective.

If this is the case with one of your applicants, ask if the nonprofit is measuring its progress and success in some way. See if they have *any* kind of standards against which they are attempting to measure their impact. There are tools that can help them. For example, can the nonprofit fully answer what Charting Impact[49] calls the following "five deceptively simple questions" (in this instance, number 4 is particularly important):

1. What is your organization aiming to accomplish?
2. What are your strategies for making this happen?
3. What are your organization's capabilities for doing this?
4. How will your organization know if you are making progress?
5. What have and haven't you accomplished so far?

When you do have an applicant who has the resources, leadership, and learning culture that has allowed it to craft, implement, review, and live by what Mario Morino calls "managing to outcomes,"[50] take advantage of it. Learn what the applicant has learned. The lessons may be valuable to others working on the same or similar missions.

---

[49] Charting Impact (http://www.chartingimpact.org/about) is a service of BBB Wise Giving Alliance, Independent Sector and GuideStar that assists nonprofits and foundations through a series of questions that result in an easy to understand report designed to communicate impact.

[50] The term is from Morino, Mario, *Leap of Reason: Managing to Outcomes in an Era of Scarcity*, Venture Philanthropy Partners in Partnership with McKinsey & Company, 2011. Morino is the co-founder of the software firm Legent Corporation and Venture Philanthropy Partners.

Measuring social impact, while desirable, is fraught with complexities and is difficult to do well. You can learn just how difficult this can be from meeting with any social scientist at your local university. You can help those you support consider better ways to measure and report their progress. But be kind. Have a frank conversation to hear what they want to measure and what stands in their way. And then consider providing support for helping them to assess their work.

For an annotated list of more evaluation tools than you'll ever want to know about, take a look at the Foundation Center's TRASI page: Tools and Resources for Measuring Social Impact at http://trasi.foundationcenter.org/record.php?SN=73.

13 | STAYING OUT OF JAIL

The Legal Stuff — Warning!
I Am Not An Attorney!

I'm no attorney, and you'll need a good one, no matter how small your foundation is. This is a specialized field. Some estate planning and most nonprofit attorneys will have the detailed information you need.

Here are the basic prohibitions against "self-dealing," which are fairly dense, somewhat complex and always seem to have exceptions. I hope this tip-of-the-iceberg outline will at least give you some questions to ask your attorney.

Self-Dealing

You cannot set up or use a private foundation to your (or any other disqualified person's) advantage — even if the foundation itself also benefits.

Sale, Exchange or Leasing of Property. Let's say your grandson works for an office supply company and offers to provide the foundation paper, pens and staples at 50% off the normal retail. Can't do it. This is self-dealing, even though it would be a nice discount for the foundation.

Leases. You have a lovely office over your home's garage that you decide you could rent to the foundation. Even if you rent it out at below market rates so that the foundation benefits, this is self-dealing. Donate the space instead. Note that any utilities you don't want to cover your foundation must pay directly to an independent third party, such as the electric company.

Lending Money or Other Extensions of Credit. Lending money or credit between a private foundation and any disqualified person is self-dealing. The exceptions are when a bank or trust that is a disqualified person makes a loan to a foundation *without interest or charge* and the foundation uses the money specifically for charitable purposes, or if a bank or trust department that is also a disqualified person provides appropriate general banking services.

Providing Goods, Services or Facilities. Similar to the Sale, Exchange or Leasing of Property (above), it is generally self-dealing if disqualified persons and the private foundation provide to each other any goods, services or facilities. The exception, again, is if it is offered by the disqualified person free of charge and it used for the exempt purposes of the foundation. Also, foundation managers, employees and volunteers can receive goods, services and access to facilities "if the value of the items provided is reasonable and necessary to the performance of the tasks involved in carrying out the exempt purpose of the foundation and is not excessive."[51] An example: meals and lodging (if not excessive) for the foundation manager that allows him or her to attend a board meeting.

Paying Compensation or Reimbursement to a Disqualified Person. This is generally self-dealing, except when you are paying for necessary, reasonable and not excessive compensation for services provided by that disqualified person, such as when a board member is also an investment advisor and they manage the foundation's portfolio, or when the disqualified person in question performs the work of the executive director of the foundation. Note: if your foundation is set up as a trust, you may compensate the trustees for their work as trustees, although you may encounter ethical issues in doing so.

Use of Foundation's Income or Assets by Disqualified Persons. This self-dealing rule is particularly tricky, so several examples follow. For example: You can't have the foundation pay an excise tax imposed by the IRS on the foundation board member for any prohibited transactions.

Another example: You're walking down the hall of your daughter's

---

[51] From IRS Website: "Acts of Self-Dealing By Private Foundations," http/:www.irs.gov:Charities-&-Non-Profits:Private-Foundations:Acts-of-self-dealing-by-private-foundation.

independent school. The headmaster sees you and casually asks if you plan on donating to the capital campaign or annual or scholarship fund. You agree to make a $10,000 donation and sign a pledge card (a legal obligation) under your own name. You cannot pay this pledge out of your foundation because this benefits you by meeting the personal obligation that you incurred during that conversation. If the headmaster applied to your foundation first, or you requested that he or she do so, your board of trustees can approve such a grant as long as it doesn't directly benefit your child and you didn't promise that the grant would be forthcoming. Of course, you can always contribute as an individual and not as the representative of your foundation.

Your foundation gave a grant to support the local theatre and it sends you tickets as a thank you. You can use one to attend a performance as a site visit where you evaluate what your grant has accomplished, but you can't ask your non-trustee spouse to attend with you. I suggest you politely send them back and buy your own tickets when you want to bring along the family — you can afford them!

Fundraising dinners similarly benefit you in that you receive a dinner — even if you don't eat it. And you can't personally pay for the dinner costs and have the foundation pay for the rest. It's best just to directly support nonprofits from your foundation and attend events and galas as an individual.

Going to the Council on Foundations' Family Foundation Conference? It's in such a nice location this year; let's bring the kids. That's fine, but unless the kids play an actual and substantive role in the operations of the foundation and attend workshops and conference sessions instead of just sitting at the pool, the foundation cannot pay for their food, travel or lodging expenses.

All private foundations are subject to these self-dealing rules for transactions with disqualified persons. Remember: Disqualified persons include the foundation's directors, officers and trustees, foundation managers, substantial contributors (see your attorney or CPA for the definition) and those persons' ancestors, spouse, children (and their spouses), grandchildren (and their spouses) and any legal entity in which any of these own more than 35%.

The rules about family staff and trustee compensation use the words "not excessive," which can be a bit subjective. Here are the facts: Yes, you can pay trustees and you can compensate family members who serve as staff. In other words, trustees can be compensated for professional (investment, legal, accounting) and grantmaking (serving as staff) services. And you can hire your son to serve as the foundation's administrator, executive director, or program officer. No, you can't pay either (trustees or hired staff who also happen to be related to you) a ridiculous amount of money or for unnecessary work or for little or no work.

How do you know what's excessive? Do a survey of other foundations your size and see which ones pay and which don't and at what level of compensation. There are a number of salary surveys (your local regional association can help you) that may serve. The vast majority of foundations (especially family foundations) do not pay their board members or trustees or even family staff. And there are those who believe doing so isn't the ethical way to approach charitable work. But there are reasons on both sides of the matter, and reading about them is useful. There are several reports and essays that can be beneficial: GMA Foundations of Boston have written some succinct articles on the subject.[52] There are some horrendous stories of abuse such as when a tiny foundation paid each of its three trustees more than $100,000 a year while they distributed a total of only $7,500 in grants. If you do engage in self-dealing, the penalties will be imposed on the disqualified person in the form of an excise tax on the amount involved. I recommend that you do your best to avoid even the appearance of self-dealing.

More Details On Distribution Requirements

I wrote about the 5% payout earlier, but this is a legal rule you must follow (and one that could change if the tax law is ever revised), so it bears repeating here.

Private foundations must distribute 5% of the average market value of their net investment assets during the previous fiscal year. You can include most administrative costs (reasonable salaries, rent, etc.) but you *cannot* include investment fees, the cost of overseeing those investments (including board or staff expenses where that issue is addressed), or excise taxes. That's why you may have heard an estate planner suggest that, to keep a private foundation from eating away at its inflation-adjusted value or corpus, you need your investments to return at least 8% or more. Obviously this cannot be guaranteed from year to year.

---

[52] See http://www.gmafoundations.com/?p=1472.

Note that if you pay out more than 5% (or exceed the average of your distributions over the five preceding tax years) you'll lower your excise tax on investment income from 2% to 1%,[53] but of course you'll also be spending more and will be required to spend more each year to keep your excise tax at that 1% level. If you fail to distribute your required payout, you may be subject to an excise tax of 30% of the undistributed amount.

There are various details that an attorney or CPA should be consulted about. You do want to avoid getting to December or the end of your fiscal year and realize that you have a lot more to grant in a rush than you thought you needed in order to meet your payout requirements. This is one reason why some donors have both a private foundation and a donor advised fund; if they haven't met their payout, rather than scrambling to get money out the door, they can make a donation to their DAF and then more thoughtfully distribute those funds in the next year.

Lobbying Restrictions

Another recap: In general, except for "self-defense" issues (potential legislation that could affect the foundation's existence, its power and duties, its tax exempt status, or the deductibility of contributions),[54] private foundations may not lobby elected legislative bodies. You may, however, educate the public about policy (as long as there's no call to action or mention of specific legislation), provide nonpartisan analysis, and, if invited in writing by the chair of an elected body, testify about an issue in which you fund. (The exception: regulatory bodies, where you can testify without an invitation and lobby.) You may also fund public charities that lobby through a general operating grant. You'll find additional information from the organization Bolder Advocacy at http://bolderadvocacy.org.

The legal and tax issues facing your private foundation can be perplexing. Always consult your attorney and your CPA when in doubt, and be in doubt whenever you aren't positive of the correct answer.

---

[53] The Council on Foundations and other grantmaker organizations have been lobbying to lower the excise tax to a flat rate of 1% for years. It was originally created to pay for the cost of the IRS' policing of foundation abuses; such policing costs significantly less than what private foundations currently pay in excise taxes. Foundations should, of course, be very careful to avoid the abuses that led to the policing and thus to the excise tax.

[54] From http://bolderadvocacy.org/wp-content/uploads/2012/05/Private_Foundations_May_Advocate.pdf

14 | BE(A)WARE: PUBLIC CHARITIES ARE A DIFFERENT BREED

Just what is a public charity? Public charities are a subset of the general category of "nonprofit organizations." Public charities are formed under state nonprofit corporation statutes and have 501(c)(3) status as determined by the IRS. They have neither shares nor shareholders and are without a profit motive. They must benefit the public directly or indirectly.

You will be making grants to public charities and it is important to understand that they are different and you may have some questions about them. Here are some answers to the following frequently asked questions that will, I hope, assist you in making thoughtful and wise donations — no matter what giving vehicle you use.

How Many Nonprofits Are There, Anyway? And Other Stats

The Nonprofit Almanac 2012 states that there are 2.3 million nonprofits operating in the United States, employing about 10% of the working population. In 2010, 62.8 million Americans volunteered to work for or at such organizations, representing the donation of "wages" worth $283.84

billion.[55] Of these nonprofits almost one million are 501(c)(3) public charities. Total estimated giving to 501(c)(3) public charities in 2012 was $316.23 billion with the majority coming from individuals.

How Are They Funded?
Where Does That $316.23 Billion Come From?

Another way nonprofits are different from for-profit businesses is where their revenue comes from. You manufacture a widget; you price it, sell it, and collect the net receipts. The more widgets sold, if each unit is priced to make a profit, the larger the total amount of revenue (and profit). On the other hand, nonprofits tend to spend more money the more clients they serve.

So where does their funding come from? The following chart sums it up well. It is interesting to note that private foundations account for only 15% of the total.

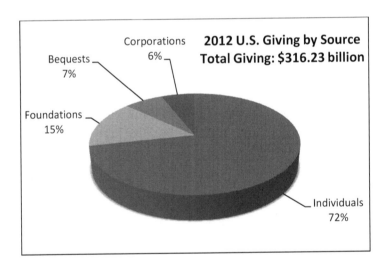

From *Giving USA 2013 Annual Report Executive Summary*

There *are* organizations that sell tickets to arts performances or museums, but they almost never are able to charge enough per ticket to cover the costs of that performance or exhibit. If they did, many people could not afford to attend. In 2010, U.S. nonprofit theatres earned less

---

[55] From Urban Institute Press, http://www.urban.org/books/nonprofit-almanac-2012/index.cfm

than half their income from ticket sales.[56] And there are nonprofits that have developed social enterprises that are businesses that bring in income while at the same time serving their mission. An example in Seattle is FareStart (http://farestart.org/), a culinary job training and placement program for homeless and disadvantaged individuals. They train their clients to run a real, operating restaurant and cater meals to disadvantaged men, women and children, and the general public. Money from the restaurant and catering service helps support the training. Another example of a social enterprise is Med25 International (http://www.med25.org/), another Seattle example — one that operates a health clinic in rural Kenya. It drilled the largest capacity clean water well in the region that doesn't require additional treatment, and it sells the water inexpensively to the community. It also just opened the doors of a mortuary (chosen by the community as its priority need) whose income is projected to completely cover the costs of the clinic within five years.

Social enterprise development is great, but not all nonprofit missions lend themselves to these activities. Also be aware that while many nonprofits don't pay federal income tax, they still may be required to pay state and local taxes, or if their earned income is not in some way "substantially related" to its mission, the earned income can be subject to taxes by the state and the IRS. There are all sorts of additional rules (and sometimes taxes) if the nonprofit is operating in another nation.

Remember, as well, that most universities and colleges and hospitals are nonprofits, so while their earned income seems substantial, their tuition and health care fees rarely cover their costs any more than typical arts organizations balance their budgets on the sale of tickets and their gift shops.

Most nonprofits receive their revenue from:

1. Gifts and bequests from individuals (the vast majority of nonprofit revenue)
2. Government contracts and grants
3. Foundation grants
4. Earned income

---

[56] See "Theatre Facts 2010: A report on the fiscal state of the professional not-for-profit American theatre," by Voss, Zannie Giraud and Voss, Glenn B., Theatre Communications Group, http://www.tcg.org/pdfs/tools/theatrefacts_2010.pdf.

The healthier a nonprofit is, the more likely its revenue comes from several of these sources, not just relying on one.

Which Causes Receive What Income?

The largest chunk of that giving goes mostly to religion (lots of people tithe), followed by education, human services, gifts to private foundations, health, international affairs, public society benefit, arts and culture, and environmental and animal causes.[57]

Another chart!

From *Giving USA 2013 Annual Report Executive Summary*

But I've Seen Nonprofit Annual Reports That Show They Have Money in the Bank, Sometimes More This Year Than Last. Isn't That a Profit?

"The IRS defines nonprofits as organized and operated exclusively for exempt purposes…and none of its earnings may inure to any private shareholder or individual."[58] This does *not* mean a nonprofit can't earn or raise money in excess of its expenses. So technically, a "profit" can inure

---

[57] From http://www.givingusareports.org/

[58] From http://www.irs.gov/Charities-&-Non-Profits/Charitable-Organizations/Exemption-Requirements-Section-501-(c)-(3)-Organizations

to the nonprofit's bottom line. What this does is allow for the nonprofit to build a healthy reserve to cover common cash flow issues. Nonprofits must plan for lean times (remember the recession?). They also must be prepared for the typical delays in reimbursement from state governments for services contracted. And they also must invest in their capacity to provide services effectively, grow to serve more people and take advantage of emerging opportunities. So it's a *good* thing that nonprofits actually earn a "profit" and accrue a reserve to meet expected and unexpected events. It just shouldn't line the pockets of the board of directors or senior staff.

I Just Joined the Board of Directors of a Nonprofit and it Seems Very Different From How Things Are Done at My Business

I bet it is. Nonprofits, more often than not, operate within a culture that is quite different from business. It stems from the nonprofits' purpose — *not* to make a profit, but to serve people who usually cannot pay for such services or to enhance the lives of the broader community. They cannot measure success by the number of widgets they sell. They are addressing difficult social problems that, if easily fixed, would have already been fixed.

Let's talk about decision-making at a nonprofit organization. In general, a public charity will have a board of directors (always uncompensated) and staff, including (or maybe only) a CEO or executive director. The executive is the operating and management leader of the organization, while the board sets executive compensation and undertakes his or her annual performance review, determines the organization's strategic vision, and acts as financial steward of its resources. In some organizations the CEO provides more visionary leadership while, especially in young nonprofits, members of the board often serve as *de facto* staff members.

The size of the agency will play a role in who is making the decisions, as will its age and stage of development (idea – startup – growth – maturity – decline – turnaround or terminate).[59] Newer organizations will attract volunteer board members who are directly connected to the mission and those volunteers will often serve in staff-like positions. For

---

[59] See Stevens, Susan Kenny, *Nonprofit Lifecycles: Stage-based wisdom for nonprofit capacity,* http://www.susankennystevens.com for a complete discussion on the stages of the lifecycle of nonprofits.

example, when I was on the board of an at-the-time relatively new chapter of a nonprofit working to seek a cure for Crohn's disease and ulcerative colitis, all of us either suffered from one of these diseases or had children or other relatives who did. Certainly that gave us perspective on the clients' needs, but we weren't necessarily well equipped to undertake other necessary functions. It can be beneficial to have board members who are well connected to the community (especially to those with the capacity to become generous donors), experienced in communications and public relations, and have legal, accounting, fundraising/marketing, and human resources skills. More mature organizations will ensure they have a board with these abilities.

So your experience on a board will differ according to the age and stage of the nonprofit. In addition, you'll often find that nonprofits are somewhat less hierarchical than traditional for-profit businesses. People come to nonprofit work from many avenues, and while some are specifically trained for this work (individuals with a master's degree in social work, public administration, not-for-profit leadership, etc.), most learn on the job or try to apply skills learned in business or elsewhere. And it's even more common for the CEOs of nonprofits to achieve their position by climbing up in their organization without broad experience with other agencies or for-profits and without training in all the CEO's responsibilities.

What is the Biggest Difference Between For-Profit and Nonprofit Culture?

Probably the pace at which decisions are made. I'm not saying that nonprofits plod along and don't work hard or long hours. Far from it. But as Mario Morino said in a Give Smart video (http://www.givesmart.org/Stories/Donors/Mario-Morino/Run-a-nonprofit-like-a-business-Why-Mario-Morino.aspx), nonprofits deal with social and life issues that are far more complex than for-profits; the work is relationship-based, subjective in nature, and takes longer to get things done. Process and full-engagement by folks around the room are very important to nonprofits, and some nonprofits value constituency involvement as well, such as low-income people on the board of an agency working to help people move out of poverty. Many factors other than the financial bottom line measure success, both for nonprofits and those who fund them.

How Else Are Nonprofits and For-Profits Different?

Compensation is one. In nonprofits, salaries tend to be lower than in for-profits and benefits are usually less (especially retirement, if any). This is often an interesting topic of discussion among foundation trustees. I've had many a client who have said something like, "If the executive director is paid more than $X, I'm not going to support them." That number is usually in the less-than-$100,000 range. I find it fascinating — and disturbing — that people expect nonprofits to do all they do without compensation rates high enough to allow a well-managed and well-run organization to better achieve its mission.

Yes, there are some nonprofits that make (bad) news because of salaries that are out of whack in relation to the size of their organization. But being a nonprofit does not mean staff *should* suffer financially. Often they do, because nonprofits are notoriously resource-poor. But when a nonprofit is successful at raising funds, I believe it is entirely appropriate to reward its employees, from the CEO on down. Otherwise, you'll have young, inexpert people cycling through regularly, eating up resources in time, training costs, and lost opportunities due to lack of experience.

What Does a Nonprofit Executive Director Do?

Often, everything! I've been an executive director for four nonprofits — three public charities and one private foundation. In two I started out with only a part-time assistant. I used to want to hang a picture of Yertle the Turtle[60] on my wall because I thought the title executive director rather grandiose for someone who, in addition to strategic visioning, board management, program design, fundraising, staff management and development, and accounting and financial oversight, was also running to the bank or post office, making copies, ordering office supplies, fixing the copier, writing all communications documents, and trying to deal with technology issues.

Think of executive directors as the chief executive officers of organizations, offering leadership and the ability to effectively implement strategies to achieve the nonprofit's mission. In particular, they need to

---

[60] Dr. Seuss, *Yertle the Turtle and Other Stories*, Random House, 1958. Yertle claimed to be "king of all he could see" which, when he was on the backs of his turtle subjects, was quite a lot; but when he fell off (after the bottom one burped), all he could see was mud.

communicate effectively, hire and successfully supervise talented staff, support and use their board of directors appropriately, and not be afraid to ask, ask, ask. For money, for partners, for advice, for volunteers, for help of all kinds.

What Does the Board of Directors Do?

Nonprofit executive directors love board members who fundraise, connect their friends and colleagues to the organization, provide sound advice and mentor them. They groan over board members who micromanage (unless invited to do so), don't see the possibilities in new ideas and improvements, miss many board meetings, or refuse to raise money.

There are any number of board "best practices" available (see BoardSource, http://www.boardsource.org) for an amazing amount of information), but here are best practices for board members summarized from the Whatcom [County, WA] Council on Nonprofits.[61]

- Reviews the organization's mission annually
- Sets and monitors policies and attends to emerging policy issues
- Reviews programs and services for links to the organization's purpose and tracks progress
- Raises money
- Reviews financial reports
- Approves budgets
- Ensures there is a clear "whistle blower" policy for employees and volunteers
- Solicits input from their communities and constituencies
- Represents the nonprofit to government, business, other agencies, funders, clients and the community at large
- Provides skills required by the organization
- Performs annual review of the executive director's performance
- Sets executive director compensation
- Hires and fires executive director as necessary

People who decide to sit on a board of directors of a public charity should make financial gifts that reflect their top tier of giving. By serving

---

[61] From http://efls.ca/webresources/WCN_best_practices_for_non-profit%20boards.pdf

as a board member they are, in effect, saying, "this organization is among the most important to me of my charitable activities." Of course, some people join boards to gain experience or a line on their résumé. And some nonprofits ask well-known people to join their board for their name recognition rather than their actual involvement. But in general, when you look over a nonprofit's board of directors, you are seeing the names of people who are extremely committed to that organization's cause. And many donors look at the board list to see who is that supportive, as one way to measure a nonprofit's quality.

The most important thing to remember? The board has the ultimate authority and responsibility for the organization.

What Are the Major Barriers to Success Faced By Nonprofits?

The lack of resources of all sorts is the major barrier. But a *Chronicle of Philanthropy* article[62] suggested others, including the following:

1. Managing 20-somethings (who seek balance in life) working alongside baby boomers (who tend to work longer hours) is a tricky task for any supervisor
2. Figuring out what is possible to measure, how to measure, and afford to measure their movement toward success...and learn from doing so
3. Keeping technology up to date and employees trained in its use
4. Staying on top of new trends such as social media and using these tools effectively

Another, more comprehensive list might include:

- Proving impact
- Crafting and implementing a business plan
- Lacking understanding whether to and how to grow and replicate
- Having little access to financial capital
- Using data to drive change and choose the best strategies
- Performing break-even budgeting
- Learning to prioritize activities toward mission accomplishment

---

[62] From *Chronicle of Philanthropy*, January 4, 2012, "Outlook," http://philanthropy.com/article/5-Challenges-for-the-Nonprofit/130193/

- Working in a leadership vacuum at both board and staff levels
- Fearing innovation and change due to worry about losing current funders

Nonprofits and for-profits face similar, but not identical issues. Nonprofits, for example, may budget on a break-even basis as their ultimate goal; no for-profit would be satisfied with that. Measurement in business might be as simple as sales numbers or the bottom line; nonprofits have a much more difficult time documenting success. Businesses can approach lenders for loans to cover capital needs, product inventory or cash flow; nonprofits work tirelessly to obtain every kind of necessary financial support. R & D is a typical line on a for-profit's financial statement or even a dedicated department. And innovating for change is built into the mind-set of for-profit CEOs, or they know they risk failure. In the nonprofit sector, change and innovation can threaten funding sources rather than enhance them.

Some foundations and philanthropists have decided that improving the ability of nonprofits to achieve their goals is where they should focus their funding, so they choose capacity building as their strategy.

What About Lobbying?

501(c)(3) public charities are also restricted in how much lobbying (influencing legislation at the federal, state or local levels) they may conduct — although they *can* lobby as long as it is not a "substantial part" of what they do and report their lobbying activities to the IRS on their 990 tax return.

A nonprofit can prove its lobbying activities are not substantial through one of two ways: a "substantial part test" and an "expenditure test."

The substantial part test involves the IRS analyzing the amount of time spent by the nonprofit's employees and volunteers as well as the amount of money it spends on lobbying activities.

The expenditure test is simpler and can be used if the nonprofit "elects to lobby," which is done by filling out a form (IRS Form 5768) and providing it to the IRS. If they elect to lobby, and a nonprofit's expenditures are less than $500,000, it can spend up to 20% of that amount on lobbying without it being considered "substantial." As the nonprofit's expenditures increase, the marginal percentage goes down.

Note that grassroots lobbying (attempting to influence legislation through an effort to affect the opinions of the general public and urging them to lobby) are limited to a quarter of the overall ceiling permitted for lobbying.[63] Note as well that 501(c)(3) public charities cannot engage in partisan political politics such as endorsing a candidate running for election.

If a public charity is found to perform excess lobbying, it can lose its 501(c)(3) status and, if it hadn't elected to lobby, it will charged an excise tax equal to 5% of its lobbying expenses, and its managers (board of directors) and CEO can also be liable to the same 5% tax.[64]

<<< >>>

Now you may have a slightly different perspective to bring when you survey the nonprofit world's terrain. The more factors you can consider, even if only in passing, the more likely you will be pleased with your philanthropic investment choices.

---

[63] From Center for Lobbying in the Public Interest, http://www.clpi.org/the-law/faq
[64] From http://www.irs.gov/Charities-&-Non-Profits/Measuring-Lobbying:-Substantial-Part-Test

15 | A SUCCESSFUL FAMILY FOUNDATION

O nce again, imagine if you will. It is now 18-months since your estate-planning attorney suggested that you might be interested in establishing your own foundation. Your own *family foundation* at that.

You took the plunge and it has worked out better than you had imagined. You consider the reasons you are feeling satisfied:

- In the beginning you carefully considered *what you wanted to accomplish by setting up the foundation*. You wanted a sense of "doing good" in your community, an opportunity to give back. You wanted to develop a family activity in which all could play a role. And, to a certain extent, you wanted the family name recognized for its philanthropic work as it already was for its business acumen.

- You already invested in good works in the community, through your own checkbook and a quarterly giving circle with friends, but, yes, your attorney was correct. You were ready for the next step.

- You and your spouse invited your two daughters, your son, and their spouses to be involved as trustees. There was some trepidation with this decision because your family encompassed a range of religious and political viewpoints (even though you thought you had raised them right).

- The family members all gathered one day last fall with the help of a facilitator to discuss what the foundation was about. *What values you all shared. What you, as a group, wanted to try to accomplish or affect in the community.* That was a lively discussion with some extreme positions, but you worked it through and settled on early childhood education (ECE). You all thought that was an area where money was always needed, and you could make some difference in the life of your community.

- With the ECE *issue focus area* decided, your next topic was *where* to give. You, your husband, and one daughter and her husband lived in one city while your other daughter and son and their spouses lived in a neighboring state. The discussion was less lively than the self-examination of values and interests that caused you to settle on ECE. The two home cities were the most sensible choice for a number of reasons, but the two most important were that: (1) You were familiar with them and knew of some of the people who could help you explore the needs of the community in your focus area; and (2) you wanted to be able to see what, if any, change your philanthropic investment yielded.

- Voilà! Your *geographic focus area* was decided!

- Then you went to work out the issue of deciding whether to accept unsolicited applications. This discussion was the wildest of them all. The consultant outlined the pros and cons and recommended that for the first round of grants, you use the more targeted approach of inviting LOIs and then applications from a few selected nonprofits. Everyone in the family (except you) wanted the experience of leaving the door open to all comers. Your vote and the consultant's advice went unheeded and it was decided to embrace the route of *accepting applications* from all interested sources that was, of course, in the *area of focus* and the *geographic limitations.*

- A long but enjoyable weekend was coming to a close with a hundred details yet to be attended to. It was quickly agreed that your husband here and your daughter in the neighboring state would begin to investigate some providers involved in ECE — the YMCA and YWCA, Boys and Girls Clubs, before and afterschool child care programs, a child care resource center that trains immigrants to provide home-based daycare, and other organizations that train and provide support to child care providers. Big jobs to be sure, but your husband and daughter have the gift of gab and enjoy being tied to their cell phones and email accounts. There was a lot to learn and they would be good and faithful researchers and reporters. You felt good that your foundation would be doing its *due diligence*.

- Happily, one of your son-in-laws is a lawyer! What a strange thing to celebrate. But he agreed to undertake the task of thoroughly *investigating the laws and regulations* governing your newly formed 501(c)(3) private family foundation to make sure you stayed on the straight and narrow. He noted that one of his colleagues specialized in nonprofit law, so if he had any questions there was easy access to additional expertise when required.

- And your daughter-in-law, perhaps with a sigh of resignation, agreed to *establish a website*, draft *an application form* for the consultant to review and, oh yeah, start trying to figure out who else was funding ECE in the community to see what could be learned from more experienced funders. *Network, network, network.*

Exhausted and exhilarated!

- The second meeting came six months later at the annual family get-together at the lake cabin. A lot of excited talk. A lot of information gathered and shared. "Did you know that this group is doing that and the results are unbelievable?" "I talked to my giving circle about what we are doing and they sent me here and there and everywhere to talk to people." "Don't let me scare you, but we have rules we have to follow." (The lawyer said that, of course.)

- Best news, worst news. The word had gotten out about your new family foundation and you already had 27 requests in hand. You and the consultant were probably correct; the *RFP or LOI* route might have been a better initially. Oh well, *mistakes often provide the foundation for success* (was that a pun?) and you will be sure to *share yours with others who follow you.*

- The third meeting came at Halloween. An application deadline had been set, but still the number had grown to 57. This is going to be hard. Your first year of grants would total somewhere in the neighborhood of $20,000. So little money. Could this still be fun?

- With your consultant, you decide that you'd attempt to limit yourselves to making only six grants this first year. Two large, around $8,000 each, and four smaller ones. There were eight possible recipients for the two large — actually there were nine but one was outside of the designated *geographic area* (not by much, but still out).

- A lot of discussion and a bit of disappointment. But the family voted to fund two community college programs, one in each of the cities, dedicated to training ECE teachers. And the four smaller donations, ranging from $500 to $1,500, were distributed to the *general operating funds* of organizations providing ECE services to low-income children and families. Your footwork and investigation has revealed that *general operating funds* were often the most useful to these non-profits. After talking with a lot of individuals involved in the work, you discovered that, more often than not, the people "on the ground" knew their needs best, and a brief review of their *financial statements* showed that most seemed well-practiced in squeezing the best value out of every dollar raised. Speaking of underpaid, you thought, those day care teachers are underpaid for sure.

- The disappointment? Your daughter had become very attached to a particular childcare provider — she signed up her one-year old to begin in the program after the first of the year. She had really wanted a small grant for new playground equipment to go the daycare center she'd chosen. Such a grant would not be self-dealing and the childcare center had even approached the foundation directly without even knowing your daughter's relationship to it. But the lawyer son-in-law reminded us all that it had been agreed that the *foundation was not our personal checkbook* and that it was important to *avoid even a chance that the public might misinterpret a grant as "unfair" in some way.*

- (Your husband, familiar as he was with *checkbook philanthropy*, made your daughter's day by sending along a personal check for the playground equipment.)

After it was over you had time to reflect. You had coffee with your family foundation consultant and expressed your pleasure with the experience. And your regrets, particularly that you had to say "no" to so many applicants. Your consultant suggested that you write short letters to those you had to decline and tell them that you would be changing procedures in the future, accepting proposals only from those invited to apply. This would save both you and them time and disappointment. He also noted that you might want to *survey the applicants* to find out how clear they found your instructions and the process of applying to your foundation. Then you could make improvements in your next round.

Accepting all applications may have turned out to be a mistake of sorts, but you did learn a whole lot about a bunch of programs and providers you might not have found otherwise. Mistakes are to be learned from. You agree to share your experience on your website and mention it at the next meeting of grantmakers in the region (which you had joined early on).

You also regretted that you had only so much money to invest in addressing the needs of young children. Your consultant suggested that you consider forming or joining something called a "funder collaborative." He said that funder or donor collaboratives could be messy and time-consuming, but that they can work effectively to channel greater funding to address important issues. They also serve to expand your knowledge of a particular issue and an opportunity to get to know the players working on the issue. This would be good, you thought, and it sure would be nice to figure out a way to make it possible for childcare providers to make something closer to a living wage.

The decision to set up your family foundation and all the toil and time-consuming discussions involved were challenging. But at the end of your first round of grantmaking, you feel much more informed and better aware about how to proceed. You're tired, but you also feel a great sense of accomplishment and look forward to effectively sharing your generosity next year.

I wrote this book after collecting questions from clients and other grantmakers. Please keep the dialogue going. Go to the contact page at Philanthropy Sherpas (http://www.PhilathropySherpas.com/contact) and use the "Do You Have a Question?" form to submit any you'd like answers to. I'll answer your questions on my blog.

— JAK

ABOUT THE AUTHOR

*J*ulia A. Kittross is the co-founder and principal of Philanthropy Sherpas, a philanthropy-consulting firm based in Seattle concentrating on making family philanthropy joyful and effective. She has more than 35 years of experience in philanthropy as a teacher, adviser, organizer, program designer, manager, grantmaker, CEO, and entrepreneur. Career highlights include working as the first full-time CEO of Philanthropy Northwest (a multi-state regional association of grantmakers), founding partner of The Giving Practice and Executive Director of the Laird Norton Family Foundation.

Trained by the National Center for Family Philanthropy to lead family foundations through its Pursuit of Excellence Assessment, Julia is also a Senior Fellow with The Philanthropic Initiative in Boston.

For more information see www.PhilanthropySherpas.com or call (206) 334-7995.

Made in the USA
San Bernardino, CA
28 October 2013